UMBILICALLY YOURS

'This book is for every mother, everywhere.'

—**Maneka Gandhi,** Former Minister of Women and
Child Development, Govt. of India

'This is an unusual publication—an ode to motherhood—written by a loving daughter.'

—**M.K. Narayanan,** Former Governor of West Bengal

'I found peace in Manisha's words because I knew they came straight from the heart of a mother who has been through it all.'

—**Megha Bajaj,** Bestselling Author and TEDx Speaker

'The book's central theme is based on the joy and privilege a woman is bestowed with on becoming a mother.'

—**Inder Raj Ahluwalia,** Travel Journalist and Author

'Manisha's own [...] journey as a Montessorian played an important role [...] in writing this book.'

—**Dame Dr Prof. Meher Master-Moos,** Founder President,
Zoroastrian College, Sanjan

'May this book serve as a guide, mentor and role model to all the expecting mothers!'

—**Dr Asha Vijay,** Founder and Medical Director of GarbhaGudi

'A guide to understand the transformative power of motherhood.'

—**Chitra Prasad,** Author, Blogger and
Correspondent, NSN Group of Schools

'It is a celebration of *Janani*—the Sanskrit word for mother, the ultimate nurturer.'

—**Dr Markandey Rai,** Chairman, Global Peace Foundation (GPF) India

'Manisha Lohia is not only a devoted mother but also a thoughtful Montessori educator whose gentle strength, deep sensitivity and rooted values reflect in every page.'

—**Gita Krishna Raj,** National Head of Physical Education Program
for Schools (PEPS), Sports Sector Skill Council of India

'I highly recommend *Umbilically Yours* to all parents.'

—**Ranjit Chaudhri,** National Bestselling Author

UMBILICALLY YOURS

SEEING, BECOMING AND BEING A MOTHER

MANISHA KANORIA LOHIA

RUPA

Published by
Rupa Publications India Pvt. Ltd 2025
161-B/4, Gulmohar House,
Yusuf Sarai Community Centre,
New Delhi 110049

Sales centres:
Bengaluru Chennai
Hyderabad Kolkata Mumbai

P-ISBN: 978-93-6156-547-2
E-ISBN: 978-93-6156-390-4

First impression 2025

10 9 8 7 6 5 4 3 2 1

The moral right of the author has been asserted.

Printed in India

I dedicate this book
at the Divine Lotus Feet of
Revered Mahātria,
who has guided me
deeper within, allowing his
words to flow through me...

To my
Matha, Pitha, Guru, Deivam—
the four forces who have always
aligned me to right living;

And to my Spiritual Parent
who has connected me to the
sacred womb...

Contents

Foreword

My mother was the strongest person I have ever known. She lived through massive upheavals and an unpredictable life, yet she was always positive, gentle, and full of happiness and grace. She made hundreds of friends and kept each one. She never criticized anyone, accepting each person for who they were. She taught me courage and the determination to forge my own path. Her favourite saying was: 'if you are good at what you do, even if it is just hammering nails in a straight line, the world will come to your door.'

I am not competitive at all; I simply do the best I can wherever life takes me—and this, I learnt from her. My mother took seven years to die of cancer—seven years of suffering, which she concealed with a smile and a home we ran to every evening, to see her and spend a happy end to the day.

When any being—human or non-human—becomes a mother, she takes on the whole world to protect her children. Even an insect will often put her babies on her stomach so that they can eat her when they are born, in order to survive. A dog mother knows she will likely lose her babies to starvation, beating and disease, yet she will defend them from passers-by at the risk of being hit herself, just to provide them with those few extra days of life.

Motherhood always brings on a primeval fear. A fear of loss, a fear of not being enough, a fear of being too late, a fear that their children will not be able to face the world happily. And yet, mothers go on. Quietly, patiently, purposefully. They don't look for glory, applause or reward. They only look for their children.

It is a kind of love that endures everything: pain, silence, even death—and still remains. It is the hope that lives inside every act of nurture, whether it's a tiny sparrow feeding her chick, a cow mourning her stolen calf or a woman standing alone against a system that failed her family. It is the love that refuses to fade— one that shapes the world through quiet courage, unwavering even in the face of despair.

There is something quietly magical about mothers—the way they remember everyone's favourite food, the way they turn ordinary days into celebrations, the way they hold entire worlds together with nothing but love and patience. This book is full of those moments. Small, unnoticed acts that carry great meaning. It reminds us that the most lasting legacies are not made of grand gestures but of consistent, gentle care.

To all those who have known the fierceness of a mother's love, or the ache of her absence, may you find yourself in these pages. May you always remember the mothers—both human and of other species—who showed you how to be brave, how to feel deeply and how to keep going, no matter what.

This book is for every mother, everywhere, in every species.

Maneka Gandhi
Activist and Former Minister of
Women and Child Development, Govt. of India

Foreword

This is an experiential testimony. Manisha Kanoria Lohia has been a part of WoW Online Writing and Healing Workshop for eight beautiful years now, and I have seen her evolve in all her roles—a loving daughter to her parents, a doting (and sometimes disciplining) mother to her son, Vedant, as a founder of iSpark and Janani, as a seeker to her Guru, as a mentee to her teachers and, of course, as an author.

Incidentally, when Manisha started writing this book, I had just conceived. She would send me chapters for review and I would eagerly read them—not just as an author–mentor, but more as a mother-to-be. While search engines would offer me multiple (and often confusing) answers to the questions I had, I found peace in Manisha's words because I knew they came straight from the heart of a mother who had been through it all.

What most appealed to me is the honesty with which Manisha has tackled every incident and how she literally becomes the voice of so many mothers and mothers to be.

Manisha's writing is simple and profound.

Her experiences are rich and insightful.

I wish Manisha many more books, and experiences, so she can keep empowering her readers.

Megha Bajaj
Bestselling Author, TEDx Speaker, Author–Mentor, Educator, Seeker and Founder, Wonders of Words

Author's Note

I am in awe of the phenomenon of human birth and marvel at how one is formed in the presence of a formless being. I wonder how life takes shape from a seed to a fully realized form within the dark chambers of a mother's womb for nine months! What emotions a mother must experience as she comes to know she has a life within her!

This sacred period is considered one of *sadhana*, which is why I write these words...

As the only daughter after four sons, I often ponder upon my mother's deep desire to have me—

What drove her to endure the pain, which she had already experienced with her sons, again?

Was it fair for her to consider going through that pain if she ultimately did not have a daughter?

Why take the chance when she was not sure of the outcome?

Her love for a girl child was so pure and intense that the higher energy—God—had to bless her with one; that was how I came into existence. I often wonder if the hardships Maa faced in desiring me and ultimately bringing me into the world were her penance. Given this, what kind of life should I strive to live?

My reverence for my mother only keeps growing with time.

I feel a deep sense of responsibility to Honour this beautiful journey that a mother goes through. I realized I should share my experiences as I have grown, my mother being a constant role model for me. By aligning herself with the laws of life, she has been blessed with abundance—something that all of us can aspire to achieve.

The idea of writing a book dawned on me as I contemplated what I could do for my mother's 80th birthday. As I delved deeper into this, I felt I could write a handbook for all mothers and mothers-to-be, who wish to live a life infused with spiritual values and holistic living.

I reflected on how the right values instilled by Maa enabled me to adapt to the changes that happened after my marriage—which I would have probably resisted otherwise. It was through these ideas that this book started to take shape.

My own journey as a Montessorian has played an important role in making me believe that there is a privilege that only a woman is blessed with—and that is motherhood. This journey, combined with my mother's teachings, brought me closer to the Divine and blessed me with a child who has been an important catalyst in further penning down my thoughts.

Motherhood has made me value and treasure children even more. Through this journey, I have realized that children are truly a gift from God, and indeed a miracle. A mother plays an important role in the upbringing of a child who grows into a responsible citizen of the world, instilled with moral and ethical values.

The deep connection I share with my Mahātria has helped me understand how my alignment with the four forces—Matha, Pitha, Guru and Deivam—plays an important role in my life, leading to the unfolding of all that is right for me. In my divine communion with God, I feel an inner strength that has allowed words to flow through me effortlessly, like a steady stream!

This book will take you deeper into understanding your own

self and help you adapt to your little one or to any relationship you encounter. You will grow in respect for children and feel a desire to hold a life within you if you are a woman, or to raise the child with the right values if you are a caregiver.

You will come to realize that, as Kahlil Gibran wrote, 'Your children are not your children. They are the sons and daughters of Life's longing for itself.'

Manisha Kanoria Lohia

Introduction

The relationship between a mother and her child is the purest of all—a divine connection that transcends time, forming an eternal, protective fence around the child. This book is unique because it speaks not only about the experience of motherhood but also honours each of our mothers. I am certain that each of you has a special place in your heart for your mother; however, in many ways, we often take this relationship for granted. I use 'granted' here in a positive connotation, as the bond between a mother and her child is one of unconditional, unquestionable love!

Choosing the title 'Umbilically Yours' carries a deep significance for me. While in the womb, the mother and child are physically connected by the umbilical cord—the vital lifeline through which nourishment, emotions and love are passed to the child. The cord is cut at birth, but the connection it symbolizes remains unbroken. The mother's love, intuition, and protective energy continue to surround her child for a lifetime and beyond, through the purity of her vibrations.

I added 'Yours' to the title because I feel every child owes a heartfelt gratitude to their mother. They are the ones who carry the child within them for nine months—so, in that sense, we are forever *theirs*—umbilically, spiritually and eternally. Hence, *Umbilically Yours!*

In this book, I have divided the journey of motherhood into three sections: *Seeing, Becoming* and *Being* a mother. The first part explores how, as a young girl, I observed my own mother and unknowingly absorbed her values. The second traces my transition into womanhood and the path towards conception. Here, I reflect on how my experiences as a Montessori educator shaped my approach towards motherhood. Finally, the third section captures how I forged my own identity as a mother—rooted in the values I witnessed growing up, enriched by my Montessori learnings and deepened by the varied experiences life has offered me.

Alongside these reflections, I have included photographs from my transformative journey—images of people who shaped me and moments that left a lasting imprint. I hope these glimpses, both visual and written, awaken memories of your own meaningful connections and inspire you to begin—or continue—your own remarkable path.

I believe this book will resonate with every woman who dreams of conceiving, and perhaps also with those who have chosen not to—maybe even inviting a change of heart. It may awaken a longing to experience the miracle of creation, to feel the sacredness of carrying and nurturing life.

That is my deepest hope: to witness that shift, that transformation in someone. Regardless of gender, I want this book to stir a deeper connection to *janani*—the Sanskrit word for mother!

PART 1

SEEING A MOTHER

In the first section of the book, I attempt to do something impossible—I am trying to put into words the story of my mother's life. Her life has been so vast, so colourful and so beautiful that confining it to 11 chapters doesn't really do it justice. And yet, I have tried to do so.

From a young age, she has been my greatest source of inspiration and the reason I felt compelled to write this book. I dedicate every word within these pages to her and the concept of Motherhood. The kind of woman she has been makes me feel even more accountable for expressing in words what I desire to express.

By now, you must be wondering, for you too, your mother is special and a source of inspiration—so what is the big deal? The big deal is to pen down your thoughts and feelings about her for the world to get inspired and to give yourself a chance to express your gratitude towards her. So why not do it? Write about her! Share her story with the world.

The greatest wealth we can leave our children is the rich values we inherit effortlessly from our parents. In this section, I have made a humble attempt to share some of my deepest learnings gained from observing Maa as I was growing up.

Mother

O Mother Dear,
I always feel you near…
Nearer than the nearest,
Dearer than the dearest,
Always with and within me.

O Mother Dear,
You taught me never to fear,
When God is near, always near.
Fear is but false evidence appearing real;
Leave fear, feel all is dear.

O Mother Dear,
Your absence brings a tear.
I wonder, when I was within you,
I felt loved, secure and protected,
Why now, this tear, which is so rare?

O Mother Dear,
Your smile is what I wear,
Your aura, the light I bear.
Your love is what makes me, ME
There is never a moment without YOU.

O Mother Dear,
You are with me through the year,
I feel you near, so there is no fear.
Though a tear wells up as my gear,
Yet I know you are forever here.

Chapter 1

Apple of the Eye

Champa Devi Kanoria's birth was a blessing to the family. Born as a chirpy little one, she spread the scent of her presence wherever she went, much like the champa flower. Her persona mirrored the essence of the flower, known for its strong, captivating fragrance.

Champa Devi Kanoria, my mother, was born in Kashmir as Champa Poddar on 24 August 1942 to Nathuram Poddar and Bimla Devi Poddar. I want to introduce her as a very passionate and enthusiastic individual who was the apple of her parents' eyes and has been the best mother to the five of us. Over the years, she has embraced many roles—mother, mother-in-law, grandmother, grandmother-in-law and even great-grandmother.

Maa, as I generally address her, excelled as a student in school, and holds many awards to her credit. She was also a talented Odissi dancer, performing on stage in school, and was my first dance guru.

A five-footer with a riot of a personality, she was a spark amongst her eight siblings—six sisters and two brothers! Born in Kashmir before India's independence, she moved to India with her family shortly before 1947. She was a keen learner, a very intelligent student and an excellent artist in all aspects (drawing, painting and dancing), and her charm shone through both her physical appearance and inner character.

Her father was a hard-working, conscientious businessman who managed many industries and mills. He was very conscious of his health and followed a strict routine of eating, sleeping, exercising, working and socializing, all while being deeply spiritual.

Her mother, a housewife, also had strong spiritual values. With eight children to look after, she hardly had time to take care of her own health. Maa grew up witnessing her parents lead a life of spiritual and ethical alignment.

As the second youngest among six sisters, she had a childhood filled with mischief and camaraderie. She also had two younger brothers, which allowed her to have the upper hand and get whatever she wanted from them. Her most adorable younger sister was her forever partner in crime. Just imagine how chaotic the house must have been with all these little ones running around and what a task it must have been for my strong grandmother to manage them all!

Being the fifth daughter in the family, and with all her elder sisters getting married at the appropriate ages for that time, it was soon time for Champa to get married too.

My grandfather was a visionary man with a razor-sharp focus; he knew exactly what he was looking for in a groom for his daughters. All he wanted was an intelligent and hard-working man who could build a family with his own integrity and strength. Money was not the only criterion for my grandfather; he believed that wealth could come and go, but men with ethical and moral values would be able to earn and support his daughters throughout life. My father, Hari Prasad Kanoria, was among the first few young men my grandfather had selected for my mother.

Back then, things were very different. Boys and girls were not allowed to speak to each other alone before the wedding. They would meet each other formally with their parents, exchange a brief glance, and in those few minutes, decisions were made as long as both families were in harmony.

However, before this moment, both families conducted thorough enquiries into each other's backgrounds, whether through the broker who had brought the alliance or a family member, with full faith in the process.

Champa and Hari met under such circumstances. The alliance was brought by a very close friend of my dad's father, who had known Champa's father since childhood. There was no looking back as the click happened between Mom and Dad in their very first meeting. Champa was 18 at that time and Hari 21—a beautiful yet tender age to embark on a lifelong journey together, learning to adapt to each other's likings while maintaining their individuality.

As Revered Mahātria says, 'We must teach the couple to become good friends for a lifetime—that is the foundation of a good marriage.'

SEEING A MOTHER

My mother—the heart of the home

PART 2

BECOMING A MOTHER

Grace in every step

Chapter 2

Marriages Are Made in Heaven

The alliance was fixed and the preparations were about to begin. As they say, 'The journey to the pilgrimage is as exciting as the pilgrimage itself.'

Hari, my father, was the oldest in his generation and the first to get married, so there was great excitement all over. As he spent his early life in a small village in Bihar, the entire village enthusiastically joined in the celebrations.

Multiple events were held to keep the excitement alive and include everyone in the joyous occasion. One memorable event was when the whole village was invited to the house for a meal. In those days, a single person did not represent a family—the entire family would come along! So you can imagine the house being thronged with about 500 village guests, along with the love, excitement and happiness they brought with them.

This was a time when one could truly experience happiness in the small things of life. For the villagers, even the act of dressing up to leave the house and go for a meal was filled with enthusiasm. The guests showered my father and the family with blessings of abundance in all aspects of life. In keeping with the saying 'Atithi Devo Bhava' (guests are akin to God), the family welcomed and treated everyone with reverence.

The union of Hari and Champa indeed blessed the house with abundance. As the oldest sibling, Hari was always looked up to with respect, love and admiration. Similarly, everyone started looking up to Maa's simplicity, graciousness and politeness. My *bua*s (aunts; Hari's sisters) were always around Champa, admiring her culinary skills and simple but elegant dressing style. My grandma was a fun-loving person and enjoyed making food and feeding others. With a cook always available to prepare lavish meals, the household was constantly buzzing with visitors who would arrive at odd hours.

My mother gradually got used to the lifestyle of her new home, which would now be hers forever. Soon she had some good news to share—the birth of my eldest brother, Hemant. The entire family was overjoyed at the arrival of their first grandson, especially my grandfather, who always wanted Hemant to be around him.

I remember Maa telling me once, 'You know, even when Hemant was asleep, your grandfather would simply sit next to him and keep observing him. He had a very strong affinity towards Hemant, and towards each one of you.'

Within a year of Hemant's birth, my second brother, Sanjeev, was born. Maa had no time to breathe; she was occupied with looking after two children and her hands were completely full. In those days, it was not easy to get helpers to look after children, so Maa had to do everything herself. A few months later, she was lucky to get a Bengali lady to help her and was finally able to get some much-needed support and rest. During this period, Dad was completely engaged in his work and hardly had any time to help Maa; the only time he got was at night and early mornings to be with his two boys.

After the birth of their third son, Sunil, one of my *chacha*s (uncle) got married, shortly followed by two of Dad's sisters. Maa had a difficult time adjusting to my aunt as she was very envious of the three sons Mom and Dad had. Back then, boys were looked upon with respect, and if one had three, it was considered a prized blessing for the parents!

Dad had six siblings, and by this time, all of them were married. The two aunts who came into the family started troubling Maa over petty things. My mother never paid heed to such things as she had her three children who brought her immense joy. She continued to fulfil her daily duties as a daughter, daughter-in-law, wife and mother, and life went on smoothly for her. Maa spent a lot of time praying and introducing her children to prayers and healthy eating. Dad was very particular about waking up early and wanted his children to follow a disciplined routine of eating, sleeping, studying and working.

Then came the birth of my youngest brother, Sujit. Although she loved her sons dearly, my mother longed for a daughter and wondered if God would ever bless her with one or keep testing her patience.

PART 3

BEING A MOTHER

The apple of everyone's eyes

My parents—newlyweds

In front of the Taj Mahal, writing their own love story

Birth of a Child

The birth of a child
Is the greatest gift
That our lives can bestow;
It brings the most exquisite
Joy that we will ever know!

The birth of a child
Is a Divine blessing,
As all days deliver happiness,
Far more than we can think;
We need the wishes of all our loved
Ones to keep going ahead in this.

The birth of a child
Is God's loving choice,
We surrender and thank Him!
For He has shared
His essence rare,
A unique star beyond compare.

The birth of a child
Is the greatest gift
That our lives can bring forth;
It brings the most exquisite
Joy that we will ever know.

All we can do is cherish,
Nurture, guide and treasure.
Hold them high, amidst all souls,
Let their light bring pleasure.
With traits so pure, they'll leave their mark,
On life's eternal sands, a rising spark!

Chapter 3

The Power of Belief

*'The beliefs you hold at the beginning
of the journey define the journey.'*

Maa was eager to cradle a baby girl after the birth of four boys; she longed to have a daughter who would complete the family. Her long-awaited desire to dress up someone as she dressed herself and the idol of baby Lord Krishna would be fulfilled if she had a baby girl. Maa has always loved dressing up and continues to adorn herself even now—she turned 82 last year, which is just a number considering she still looks as young as 50!

Clothes and jewellery have always attracted her. Yet I have seen her carry herself with utmost simplicity and elegance, without ever overdoing it. As a result, she always stands apart from the crowd. On the other hand, the idea of dressing up her boys overwhelmed her...

Yet, Maa being Maa, she decided to dress up Sunil Bhaiya like a girl one day when he was four years old. She borrowed a small *lehenga* from one of her friends who had a daughter of the same age. Along with the lehenga came the accessories, and soon, there he was—all dressed up like a girl! I am sure that if he had been old enough to understand, he would have protested. But that wasn't the end of it—she was fond of taking photographs and requested my youngest uncle to take a few.

This incident became one of the many reference points in

the family for Maa's desire to have a daughter—everyone realized how much she longed for one. I believe the Universe heard it too, with the mass vibrations of so many people wishing for a girl child for Maa as well!

However, the decision-makers were my parents and God. After Sujit, Mom and Dad decided not to have any more children, as taking care of four boys was proving to be quite a task. Dad arranged for Maa to undergo a procedure to prevent further pregnancies.

On the day of the appointment, as they were about to step out of the house, my grandma saw them and casually asked where they were going.

How could Maa say anything except the truth! She has always taught us to be honest. My father knew that things would become difficult if Grandma came to know where they were heading. While Dad was working this out in his mind, Maa meekly and coyly confessed, 'Maa, we are going to the doctor. He has arranged for a surgery so that I do not conceive again.'

My grandma was taken aback and resisted the very thought of Maa undergoing surgery at such a tender age. In those days, surgeries were considered extreme and were only undertaken when deemed 'urgent' for one's life.

She gently yet very sternly told my father, 'Hari, why are you doing such a thing without asking me? Children are God's blessing. So what if you get one more? Do not indulge in such heinous acts. I will pray for Champa to have her long-desired daughter. Mark my words, the fifth one born to both of you will be a baby girl. Champa, please go back inside, and Hari, go to work.'

The blessings of a mother can never be turned down. Her silent prayers and whispers resonated with the universe and in due time turned into a reality.

My mother's earnest yearning and my grandmother's reassuring words could not be turned down by God. Four years after Sujit's birth, Champa cradled a baby girl in her arms. My arrival was a divine calling from the craving heart of the pure soul of a mother.

My name, Manisha, reflects this divine connection: 'man'—heart and 'isha'—like God.

After my birth, my eldest brother named me Hemlata ('hem' from 'Hemant' and 'lata' meaning a delicate creeper)—one he would protect as his own tender little one. It showed his innocent love as an elder brother, who felt responsible for the little life in his arms.

This name was even registered in school and other official documents for a long time, until my *maasi* (aunt; mother's sister) thought the name was too traditional and might not resonate well in a contemporary school setting. She changed it to Manisha. How wise she was! I can hardly imagine introducing myself as Hemlata while growing up—I shudder at the very thought of it! Many thanks to Maasi for changing my name—though I have a soft spot for the name lovingly given by my brother, who continues to dote on me.

I hold on to the phrase 'The beliefs you hold at the beginning of a journey defines the journey,' as this worked wonders for Maa in her quest to bring a girl child into this world.

◆

Personal note: One incident I fondly recall and would like to share here as a funny anecdote happened a few years back when I met the nurse who had delivered me. I was the only one among the five siblings to have been born in a hospital. Prior to my birth, my brothers were born at home, which was the norm in those days. A hospital delivery was typically associated with some complications the mother might have faced during childbirth. For Maa, it was to stop the process of conception.

The nurse who first held me was entrusted with breaking the news to Maa that she had delivered a baby girl. Beaming with happiness, the nurse headed towards my mother, who was still groggy from the delivery and the procedure that followed to ensure she couldn't conceive again.

The nurse told her, 'Champa, see, you have given birth to a daughter!'

Semi-conscious, she thought that the nurse was lying to her to spare her the disappointment of yet another son. In her daze, she whacked the nurse on her face and exclaimed, 'You are lying to me! I know I cannot have a girl!'

But in her heart, she probably knew that it had to be a girl this time. What a grand entry I made into the world! And what a grand moment for my angel nurse who helped bring me into the world!

Sanjeev and Sunil in their toddler days

Sanjeev and Sunil in their toddler days

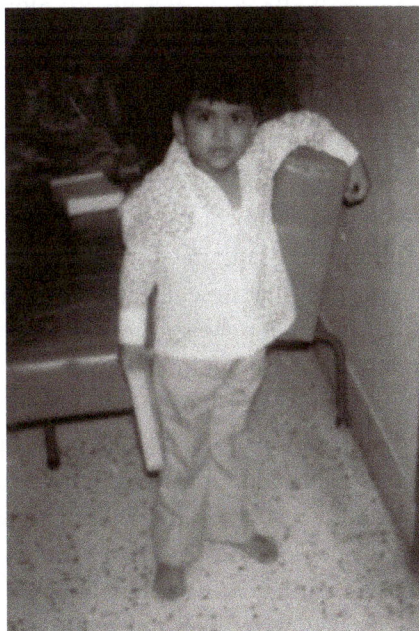

My brother Sujit

Chapter 4

The Making of Us

'Children learn much more from what they see than what they hear.'

Maa's plate was full now—to look after five children, that too four boys and a girl, was not easy! Yet, she moved along happily, caring for each one of us in a way we could individually connect with her. I must re-emphasize this: she connected with each one of us—which is very important as every child is different, and only a mother knows 'that' special way to bond with her child. A big salute to this beautiful concept called motherhood, which God has so kindly bestowed upon women.

Raising five children with just one helper was not easy, but Maa did it with unflinching faith in God and in herself, along with Dad's tireless support. At that time, Dad was extremely busy with work as he was setting up a new venture—a flour mill. My birth coincided with this breakthrough in his career. He was offered the opportunity to revive a defunct flour mill originally established by the British that had shut down due to lack of manpower. Hence, I was considered to be the Lakshmi of the house.

Dad's unavailability at home till late hours often put Maa in a very challenging situation. Her children were growing up and, as I have mentioned earlier, raising four boys was a Herculean task. They were always quarrelling and fighting. Maa recalls an incident with a sparkle in her eyes:

'Sanju was the naughtiest of all; he would go around scolding everyone in the family or in the building if he felt they had misbehaved. He demanded discipline and good behaviour from all, and if we failed to meet his expectations, he would reprimand us.'

Maa used to call him Kamsa when he was young. One day, he ran away from the house after breaking a mirror, fearing punishment. He sat under a tree till late in the night, certain that no one would find him. When Dad returned from work, Maa asked him to look for Sanju. Knowing his usual hiding spots, Dad easily found him. Naughty Sanju had no hint of guilt and simply looked at Maa with a twinkle in his eyes, as if his actions were entirely acceptable!

Maa fondly says, 'I simply hugged him and then fed him, as he had disappeared for hours without a morsel.'

She realized that scolding alone wouldn't help; the self-awareness would have to come from within him. Sanju, now 62, is an ardent devotee, a meditator and, above all, one of the leading liver transplant surgeons in the world. It is a testament to how a mother's patience and belief can transform even the naughtiest child into a leader with strong values and a heart full of peace.

On the other hand, Maa was always concerned about me as I was the youngest and most fragile of her five children (a sentiment she holds to date). She felt scared that I would be bullied by my brothers, especially Sanjeev and Sujit, so she always kept me close to her in my growing years.

Her surrender to God was so complete and unwavering that in moments of distress, all she would do was sing and dance with total abandon in front of her Lord, regaining her peace. I remember seeing her in tears in the puja room. Her intense bhakti resonated deeply with me, and I often found tears rolling down my own cheeks as I observed her.

As a child, I could not fully understand her emotions, but I somehow maintained composure and never bothered her during such times.

I often wonder how I was able to sense such things as a child.

Even now, thinking of those moments gives me goosebumps. Children in their early years are very sensitive—they may not have the words to express their feelings, but they intuitively understand the emotions of those around them, especially their close ones, like their mothers.

Meanwhile, Dad grew busier by the day and we hardly saw him during the week. Our daily routine of waking up, studying, eating, playing and sleeping on time was carried on under Maa's planning and supervision. She had a daily schedule for each of us and ensured we followed it.

Hemant, being the eldest, was able to take care of himself quite well and helped his younger brothers too. But as he advanced in school, he also had to dedicate enough time to his studies and learn the nuances of business from Dad.

Maa eagerly waited for the weekends when she could breathe a sigh of relief and pack us off with Dad to the flour mill on Saturdays. As I look back, I am sure this gave her some time to relax and unwind. For us, Saturdays were for chilling and *masti* time with Dad—a *masti ki paathshaala*—where we could learn and have fun! We looked forward to such days when we could witness the hard work our dad had to put in for us to live a comfortable life!

Our flour mill was one of the biggest in India, supplying flour to major clients. Dad was successful in reviving the mill, which had been handed over to him by his father. My grandfather had seen immense potential in his son Hari, which he had not seen in any of his other sons.

Although I strongly believe a mother's role has the strongest impact on a child's formative years, for us, both Maa and Dad played integral parts in shaping who we are today. Now in their 80s, they continue to inspire us with their active, independent lives.

The beginning of my story

This Cosmic Drama of Life

Entrain me…
O Lord, in this cosmic drama of life,
Where naught exists but you and me.
Where a divine touch from Thee transforms me—
Where I, who am blessed to be Thy fragrance,
Spread Thy divine touch to all souls I meet;
Like hay fire, spreading by its very nature...
I too shall spread the fire of love with grace, to all who
I meet.

Dissolve me…
O Lord, in this eternal drama of life,
Where the seeker and the sought exist not,
And a mere union of sorts happens with oneness.
In this oneness, everything fades away—
A feeling of nothingness (*shunya*) descends!
A heavy load seems to be lifted,
Which we realize is the weight of the ego within us.

'Forget me…
Not, O Friend, in this *maya* of life,' a voice echoes.
'I have given you this precious gift of a human life;
You have no right to waste it in complexities or gossips.
These arise only when you move away from Me.
You and I are never apart,
It is your thoughts that create the distance.

Hold me close within, through devotion,
As We will keep dancing this cosmic dance of life!'

To me...
This cosmic drama of life is an eternal unfolding,
Where I feel I am nothing but Him,
In merging with Him, I find nothingness.
I carry this union with me in all tasks—
I realize life in itself is a process, act we must,
worthy ones,
Feel obliged that He created us to create—
Create through words, thoughts and actions
That touches all hearts to take them within,
To make each feel one with their One within!

Chapter 5

Making Each Day Count

'Today is the first day of the rest of your life.
Make it count. Every day matters...'

I have always seen Maa live her life with boundless energy and enthusiasm. She embraces each day as if it were the best day of her life, and she has taught us to do the same. Even with her hands quite full, managing five children and the household chores, she always took out the time to pursue her passion for the arts. A natural artist, Maa always excelled in drawing, painting, singing and dancing.

Even at 82, Maa continues to live with the same zeal. Now, she writes and curates her own bhajans, even learning a few dance steps to accompany them. She celebrates festivals like Holi and Krishna Jayanti with cultural performances and invites her close friends and family to join in the festivities.

One carpe diem moment I hold dear occurred when I was in grade three. Maa would always decorate my music book with her drawings and paintings, matching the lyrics of the songs. On one occasion, she drew a beautiful pussycat sitting in a garden. When my music teacher saw the drawing, she smiled and asked me who had made it. When I told her it was my mom, her smile widened.

On parent-teacher day, when Maa met the teacher, she told my mother, 'Ma'am, the cat's eyes looked so real I felt it was talking to me!'

Maa's eyes sparkled with delight at the unexpected appreciation; she had made the drawing without expecting any applause.

This is Maa's way of life—living every moment to the fullest, without desires or expectations.

From a young age, each one of us was taught to approach life as if every day was the first day. We have to make it count as everyday matters. Watching Maa, Papa and all my brothers live this mantra, how could I not have ingrained it in my mind! As I pen these words, I feel a deep 'Aha!' at the richness of this upbringing and a fervent desire to spread its fragrance to all!

Dad's sincerity, love, enthusiasm, energy and intelligence shone through as we saw him working diligently even on Saturdays, except for the one hour during lunchtime that he carved out for us. The five of us and Dad would have lunch in the dining area near his cabin at the factory. We would be extremely excited to share this time with a cool, loving father, who was also demanding in his own way. We laughed, talked, fought with and, most importantly, loved each other.

During the week, Dad would wake us up early, make us do yoga with him and ensure we had a healthy breakfast with milk, fruits and nuts. He never hesitated to help Maa in the kitchen or get us ready when we needed help. Maa, meanwhile, would adorn the puja room, bathe our little idol of Krishna and dress him in fresh clothes and jewellery. Each morning, as we prayed before leaving for school, we knew our Krishna would see us off with a radiant smile.

The most beautiful part of our morning schedule that I cherished was the devotional songs that reverberated throughout the house as we left for school. It would be a combination of Hari Om Sharan's and Bengali bhajans, Meera Bai's compositions and Anup Jalota's melodies. Somehow this soulful ambience was etched in the five of us, and as we grew older, we have attempted to carry this tradition into our own families, hoping to create similar memories for our children.

This foundation instilled a deep responsibility within me, shaping my perspective on nurturing and guiding children.

◆

A phrase of my revered Guru that resonates deeply is: 'Not like this; like this.'

This simple yet profound approach reminds us to guide children with positive reinforcement, saying: 'Not like this; let us do it like this.' Such affirmations form positive patterns in young minds, and this is exactly what Maa did with us. She set clear expectations, reinforced them with positive affirmations, and whenever we failed to do the task at hand, she provided loving feedback for us.

This, I believe, is what 'strict love' is—it makes us act in the appropriate way. Believe me, my dear readers, Maa never took any parenting courses to achieve this. Her instincts as a mother propelled her to make the right choices and act accordingly. This innate wisdom is something each one of us is capable of tapping into, through our *atma shakti*.

That is the spark that inspired me to write this book. The words flowed naturally—by the grace of Revered Mahātria— fuelled by the love and lessons imparted by my extraordinary Maa.

Chapter 6

Careful Steps, Divine Blessings

'When we do our best, God takes care of the rest.'

The children were growing up pretty fast, and Dad's flour mill business was taking most of his time and energy.

Bengal Flour Mill was a joint initiative, with Dad's brothers and their uncles sharing the profits. However, Dad was the only person working tirelessly; it was his natural instinct to work, work and work. He was guided by the philosophy: 'Keep working till the end; there is no retirement. Do not think of results—just do your best. When we do our best, God takes care of the rest.' This mantra seeped into Maa and each one of us. What a life it has been, as we grew up believing in this philosophy!

As I reflect now, as the mother of a 27-year-old son, I marvel at the Herculean task it must have been to raise five children, each at different milestones of growth. But even as I write this, I realize I am wrong—in those times, no task was considered 'Herculean'; every task was a choice one performed happily, especially in respect with the children one birthed.

I apologize for using the term 'task'; modern parents often see raising children as a task—a monumental responsibility; many even choose not to marry and have children. But in our family, the five of us grew up together. The older siblings took care of the younger ones, while the younger ones learnt by observing the elders.

Maa gave each one of us individual attention and encouragement. She gave her best to nurture our mental, psychological, emotional and physical well-being. Today, as I evolve in maturity, I recognize how profoundly this has strengthened my being. A strong sense of self has made the doing much easier, ultimately aiding in my becoming.

Mentally, Maa is a tough woman, though she undoubtedly faced vulnerable moments living in a large joint family. Her unwavering faith in God, coupled with Dad's support, helped her overcome all situations as she was always willing to welcome the next phase of her life. Her resilience has left an imprint on our minds and lives as well.

Psychologically, she made sure to use affirming words and statements so that we could imbibe the same. Emotionally, Maa is a rock; even when life threw her unexpected challenges, she bounced back with renewed enthusiasm and vigour. I vividly recall her spending hours in the prayer room, adorning our idol of little Lord Krishna, singing bhajans and chanting shlokas. This was her sanctuary—the wellspring of her courage and strength.

Recently, my dear friend and yoga mentor Shoba shared a profound insight: 'The more we advance in spirituality, the more we are faced with tougher situations. This is only because God loves us deeply and knows what to give to each one of us, according to our capability to handle the situation.'

Maa exemplified this beautifully. Her co-sisters envied her for having four sons, who they knew would do very well in life and support Maa. They often troubled Maa by locking the kitchen when she needed to prepare food for us.

Maa was very particular about giving us enough fruits, vegetables and milk, even if other luxuries were compromised. She would make healthy snacks for us at home, which were tailored to our tastes and palate.

When my aunts locked Maa out of the kitchen, she turned to Krishna. She would retreat to her room and dance with complete abandon to Meera's bhajans, offering her worries to her beloved

Lord. These were her most vulnerable moments, as she realized she would not be able to provide for the physical well-being of her children; only her Krishna could help her during such times.

Dad was always there to support Maa and find solutions for problems rather than complain about them. He set up a small pantry on the veranda where Maa could keep fruits, milk and snacks for us. This solution, to Maa, was Krishna's way of helping her.

It was very evident to us that Mom and Dad lived every aspect of their lives through *seva* to the Lord. Raising us was seva for them as they had brought us into existence. They taught us that for every situation, there is always a solution or a way out if we look for it—a lesson thus deeply embedded in our growing minds. To raise us with the right values was the best they could have done for us, so how would God not take care of the rest then!

Maa always believed and reminded us that 'to receive God's grace, we must do everything to the best of our capacity; beyond that, God will take care'.

I feel blessed to have a mother like her; I have learnt so much from observing her. She is always with her five children, carrying us in ways we may never fully comprehend!

Ultimately, I feel the purest intent a parent should have for their child is the faith that they will do well in their life. With that intent, success becomes inevitable. It has happened and keeps happening for millions of folks around the globe, who have lived with this intent.

Maa standing before her Lord in quiet reverence

In Krishna's court, we danced as one

I Am His Instrument

I am His instrument;
He chooses me to do His work,
To spread His fragrance of love
To one and all who come under my purview.

This life is blessed by God,
A reflection of His grace,
This life is a journey I tread upon,
Guided by unflinching faith in Him.

He plans every move for me,
With my maturity, sometimes I ask,
'Why me?' With His grace I realize
Why me! Why does He love me so much!

The more and more I keep surrendering,
The more and more I keep drawing Him
Within every cell of this human body,
Which reverberates with His energy alone.

I sometimes wonder how this happens,
This wondering goes on, it never stops;
The more I wonder, the more He blesses with,
And I keep evolving and growing in Divine love!

Whatever I do, I can feel the presence of God;
Whatever I touch is touched by His touch.
I lose the cravings of all sense pleasures.
All I feel is Him, His grace, His radiance.

I soak, dissolve and immerse in Him,
Doing nothing of my own accord.
He does it all through me,
For I am but His instrument,
A vessel in His divine *leela*.

Chapter 7

Life Paves the Way for a Resolute Soul

It was a difficult period when my grandma passed away at the age of 55 due to heart failure. Everything changed in our family after that; there were insurmountable challenges at both home and on the business front.

After all the hard work Dad had put into Bengal Flour Mill, it was given away to his brothers and uncles. Unfortunately, they could not look after it with the passion and zeal that Dad had. Hemant had just turned 17, and with his help, Dad took over another financially unstable mill in Kolkata, which he named Sri Radha Krishna Flour Mill.

After the demise of my grandmom, my aunts started troubling Maa even more; my granddad, an otherwise calm and patient man, succumbed to whatever was happening. We moved to our new house, where my father's two brothers and two uncles would also be staying. We had separate floors for each family and also separate kitchens, which gave Maa the flexibility to plan our meals tailored to our individual choices and needs. We loved eating whatever she cooked for us; everything she prepared was made with love, so it all tasted delicious.

With more comfort came more situations. Our financial condition had deteriorated, and Dad had to start afresh. My maternal grandfather gave him a small space in his office—the veranda—from where Dad started his financial journey again, with a few hundred rupees in his pocket, a 17-year-old son and an old cashier (who vouched that he would never leave Dad, and his son continues to work for us even now). Dad did not want my granddad to feel obligated to help him out, so he paid rent for using the veranda. That was Dad—what he still is…

Maa was no less than Dad; both of them complemented each other. She saved money from wherever she could and used it judiciously, spending only what was required. It must be said that they never for once compromised on our education or health.

Those were very difficult years for Dad and Hemant as they worked tirelessly to set up the two flour mills—one in Kolkata and the other in Krishnanagar. Through consistent, self-motivated and intelligent efforts, along with complete faith and surrender in God, father and son were able to stabilize our financial situation. With the influx of funds, we were able to move to another office space.

Hemant had to set aside his desire to pursue postgraduation or become a chartered accountant to support Dad in growing the business.

When Hemant turned 21, our grandfather became keen on getting him married. A strong bond existed between them and he convinced Hemant to get engaged as soon as a suitable proposal arrived.

Maa was very happy to welcome her first daughter-in-law into the house, thus commencing her next phase as a mother-in-law. However, like any traditional Indian family, certain norms were deeply rooted. Although Maa was different, she was still a little orthodox when it came to defining my relationship with my sisters-in-law. She insisted they address me as 'didi', as was the custom in a typical Marwari family set-up.

Being nine years younger, I found it hard to accept someone older addressing me as '*ji*' or 'didi'. I voiced my objections as I would eventually have four sisters-in-law, who would all be older than me. Maa struggled to accept this change at that time and still does. I, however, am at peace because this has given me the freedom to establish my individual relationship with each one of them.

Over time, both of us have found a middle ground and peacefully moved ahead. This reminds me of Mahātria's words: 'Human beings are a product of their past conditioning.' I have come to respect Maa's thought process and the values shaped by her own past conditioning and experiences.

Dad's advice to Maa during this time was profound. He told her, 'Never say anything negative about your daughter-in-law to Hemant. He will feel very sad and it will put him in a conflicting situation. Whatever issues you have with her—sort it out directly but stay calm and patient. She has grown up in a different environment and it will take time for her to get tuned to our family—as it did for you. You must support and understand her; this way, you will always win the hearts of your sons and daughters-in-law-to-be.'

Maa took every word of Dad to heart and indeed contributed towards a happy, harmonious family. Over time, she welcomed four more daughters-in-law with the same grace and understanding.

Through it all, Maa's never-let-go attitude has become a beacon for us. Even as a child, although I could not fully understand, I sensed the quiet strength and resilience in her every action. These lessons, absorbed subconsciously, shaped me into a resolute soul, ready to face life's situations with grace.

Thank you, Maa and Papa, for making me 'me'—a unique individual with distinct characteristics shaped by both of you and God!

Chapter 8

And Love Expands Our Family

'Go as far as you can see; when you reach there,
He will take you further.'

As our family began expanding with the arrival of new members, we embarked on the journey of welcoming the third generation, which started with the birth of Hemant's daughter, Siddhi. Her arrival brought immense joy and excitement, especially to Maa, who always had a very strong affinity towards a girl child. When my niece was born, she celebrated Siddhi's birth with the same grandeur as one would for a baby boy.

Maa had welcomed her first daughter-in-law with a lot of warmth and grace, guided by Dad's advice to nurture harmony. My *bhabhi* was only 18 when she got married, and she adapted easily to our family. She came with strong family ethics and blended well into our household of five siblings.

Before long, within just a year, Bhabhi was expecting her first baby. We were all very excited, as we had never experienced the arrival of a newborn so closely before. The day my niece was born is etched deep in my mind. I was only 11 when Siddhi was born, and our relationship blossomed like that of sisters—a connection that remains strong to this day.

Siddhi's birth brought mirth, joy and excitement to every corner of the house. Our grandfather was super excited to hold his first great-grandchild, showering her with love.

His sudden passing in 1986, while climbing a mountain for *darshan* at our family deity's temple in Rajasthan, was a profound loss for all of us. He suffered a heart attack and collapsed immediately. My youngest uncle, who was accompanying him, brought Granddad back to Kolkata for his last rites.

Granddad was only 70 when he passed away, and his departure left a void in the family. For months, we felt disoriented, struggling to come to terms with the absence of his unwavering love and guidance. Each day, Granddad would give each of his grandchildren (13 of us) money to save in our piggy banks, while Siddhi, his first great-grandchild, received extra. Although she was only a year and six months old when he passed away, she still has faint memories of him.

When genuine people touch the hearts of children with love, it creates a carpe diem moment for them. They may not be able to express it in words, but they always hold on to these special moments, even from a young age.

With Hemant by his side and his unflinching faith in Maa Kali, Dad pushed through the insurmountable challenges in business, holding on to his moral values and spiritual strength.

In 1987, Maa initiated the next chapter by seeking a match for Sanjeev, who was preparing to leave for the UK to pursue a career as a liver transplant surgeon. No one in our family had ever gone overseas to work or study, and Maa was very nervous about Sanjeev. His adventurous spirit made her anxious, but she trusted that his kind heart would win over anyone and everyone.

Sangita, his bride, came from Jakarta and fit seamlessly into our family with her grace, poise and soft-spoken demeanour. Maa's love and acceptance allowed Sangita to adapt to the changes smoothly, and with two daughters-in-law, Maa's nurturing presence continued to bloom.

In 1988, the birth of Mukund, Sanjeev and Sangita's son and our first nephew, was a blessing and brought even more joy to our growing family. Slowly, Dad's business started stabilizing and Sunil, our third brother, joined Dad and Hemant in its expansion.

Sanjeev's plans to move to the UK left the responsibility of the business's growth with Hemant and Sunil, but the family's faith in God's plan remained unshaken. Both Maa and Dad lived by the principle of 'going as far as you can see, and when you reach there, God will guide you further'. Their spiritual maturity helped them navigate the highs and lows with grace, teaching us that life's challenges are part of God's divine play. They prayed for strength and wisdom, believing that while God never lets go of us, it is often we who forget Him in the distractions of a worldly life.

A happy, growing family

Love

Love is when I feel one with you,
When I no longer see 'you' or 'me'.
Love is seeing tears in your eyes
And feeling them well up in mine.

Love is beyond expressions,
Love does not have boundaries,
Love does not say 'I love you' to one
And turn away from another.
Loving unites 'you' and 'me' forever as one,
Where there is no 'you', no 'me',
But always a feeling of 'us' and 'ours'.

How do I write of love,
When love is all I feel?
Can it ever be defined through
Expressions or paragraphs, I wonder!

Love can never be expressed.
The more I try to put it into words,
The further I stray from its truth.
Yet the less I say,
The more deeply I feel it—
In smiles that shine through tears,
In silence that speaks volumes.

I pray to my God every moment,
Communing with God within—
'My God, my Divine Lover,
Teach me to love as You do.

'Always feeling the pain of others,
Always doing what THEE guides me to do,
Always putting others ahead of myself;
For in love, there is no "me", no "you",
There is only "we".

'In love, there is no ego,
For ego erases You from our hearts.
Help me love purely, I pray to love purely,
As You love us all.'

Chapter 9

Lessons from a Tragedy

'In the sway of emotions, intelligence does not work—so refrain from action or decision-making.'

The family was expanding from seven members to eleven, and it would continue to grow even further as the younger two brothers got married. The advantage of having a big family lies in the rich interactions with members of different ages and personalities, all under the same roof.

Navigating relationships within a large family— four brothers and their wives, each shaped by diverse past conditioning—helped me become emotionally resilient and make intelligent choices, guided by the values imparted by my parents, brothers and life itself.

Returning to the story of my mother—living in a large joint family teaches invaluable lessons and Maa, shaped by these experiences, was an embodiment of those learnings. Yet, like all humans, she would become emotional at times. Dad, always her steadfast partner, provided the insight she needed to respond to situations calmly and gracefully.

In 1988, Sunil Bhaiya got married, and by 1990, the family had grown with the births of two more grandchildren, Anant and Raghav. As the family expanded, I found immense joy in being surrounded by children, while for Maa, it meant growing responsibilities. She was constantly busy, welcoming her grandchildren and meticulously taking care of her daughters-in-law during their post-delivery recovery by providing them with healthy, nutritious meals.

One remarkable trait of Maa is how her spiritual routine remains unaffected, no matter the circumstances. Her connection with God—the 'Z' factor in her life—infused her with boundless strength that enabled her to nurture a growing family with peace and love.

◆

In 1989, a drastic event changed the course of our lives. Hemant and Sunil met with a major car accident while returning home one rainy morning after playing squash and tennis. A truck collided head-on with their Maruti 800.

In that moment of peril, Hemant felt a divine presence urging him to act. He saw an apparition of God telling him to jump out of the car and push Sunil to safety. Despite his own injuries, Hemant managed to drag Sunil, who was unconscious, into a taxi and bring him home.

I will never forget the sight of Hemant at our doorstep, bleeding and calling out, 'Maa, Maa! Sunil…Sunil…'

I was playing with Siddhi in the drawing room and was the first to see him. I rushed to the puja room to alert Mom. The moment she saw their state, she fainted. For Maa, Hemant was like her Rama; the thought of something happening to him was unbearable.

I took it upon myself to find my uncle for help, as there was no one around me to take decisions. My sister-in-law was also up and about by then. By God's grace, we managed to take Hemant and Sunil to a private hospital with the help of my uncle and other family members. Dad, who was on his morning walk, was directed to the ICU upon his return.

The following weeks were a trial of faith and endurance. Both brothers underwent multiple surgeries. Sunil remained in a coma for a week due to internal trauma, while Hemant required extensive medical care. After four weeks, by the grace of God and the strength of Maa's convictions, they began to recover.

This accident was a transformative moment for the entire family. Maa became a pillar of strength for each one of us, consoling our emotions and needs during this situation.

Despite her emotional upheaval, she lived by the principle that embodied the lesson: 'In the sway of emotions, intelligence does not work, so refrain from action and decision-making'. Looking back, it feels as if God was guiding us to make the right decisions; how else could the brothers have survived such a horrific accident?

Through these trials, I absorbed invaluable lessons from Maa, which got embedded in my subconscious forever. It gave me the resilience to live my life with the same integrity and peace that I have witnessed in my mother. Daughters tend to emulate their mothers, and for me, my maa is a living role model.

Me with my parents—their greatest joy

Hemant and Sunil—emerging triumphant among all hurdles

Chapter 10

Owning My Choices

'My life is my responsibility; no blaming is allowed.'

The accident had deeply shaken the family, but it also brought everyone closer. The brothers recovered and were ready to embrace a new chapter in their lives.

As Revered Mahātria says, 'Every end is a new beginning'— I have always seen Maa live by this philosophy, regardless of the circumstances.

It was around this time that SREI (meaning *shreshth* in Sanskrit; supreme) Infrastructure and Finance Limited was established by Hemant and Sunil.

Maa continued her role as a mother, mother-in-law and grandmother with unwavering dedication. In 1993, Sujit got married. Prior to that, Maa tried convincing me to do the same, but I refused. In my heart, I was already married—to my Krishna. I had no other desires and was determined to pursue my ambitions. My plan was to go to the UK for higher studies; with Sanjeev Bhaiya already there for his Fellowship of the Royal College of Surgeons (FRCS) degree, Dad would readily agree to let me go there. But, as they say, life had its own plan for me.

Maa grew busier managing the household and her expanding family. By now, she had four daughters-in-law (though one lived in London) and four grandchildren. She radiated joy and ensured everyone felt included and cared for.

Despite her increasing responsibilities, Maa never neglected her own health or spiritual practices. She maintained a disciplined routine—waking up early, sleeping on time, eating healthy, working efficiently and dedicating herself to her daily puja.

Maa's love for dressing up and cooking was evident in her everyday life. She took great joy in making pickles and papadam for the family, involving her daughters-in-law, to pass down these traditions. Every morning, she would dress elegantly after her bath and head straight to her puja room—rituals she continues to follow even now.

On days when I feel low, I close my eyes and visualize her. I remind myself of her energy and resilience with the mental affirmation: 'energy on the move'. Instantly, I feel reinvigorated, ready to welcome the day with the same vigour.

What I admire most about Maa is her ability to live her life responsibly—first for herself and then for the many roles she plays in the family. I have never heard her complain about anything or anyone. Her strength came from her unwavering devotion to God. She never blamed anyone for anything, choosing instead to align herself with the divine and draw her strength from within.

Dad, at that time, was deeply engaged in helping my brothers set up their businesses, always supporting and guiding them. Together, Mom and Dad exemplified how to fulfil life's responsibilities with balance and poise. Watching them, we learnt to live our lives with the same alignment.

◆

I had just completed college in 1993, and Maa was keen to get me married. As always, she was concerned about my well-being; I lived in my own little world—sometimes lost in my Krishna devotion, other times driven by my ambitions and aspirations. Looking back, now as a mother myself, I can empathize with her feelings. Whether raising sons or daughters, parents naturally want the best for their children.

I was only 22 and not too old for marriage, but times were different back then. Girls were married between 16 and 18, and even my younger cousins had already settled into their married lives. Maa's desire to see me married stemmed not only from societal norms but also from her deep affection for me.

Finally, what Maa had been longing for came to fruition. Like every mother, she wished to see her daughter married into a loving, reputable family and settled happily. In our culture, *kanyadaan* ('kanya' meaning 'daughter' and 'daan' meaning 'to give away') is considered the greatest of all blessings. Maa had always wanted to experience this sacred act. She had heard from her mother that by performing this ritual, she would accumulate good karma in her life.

In the *Ramayana*, King Janaka describes giving away his daughter Sita to Lord Rama as the highest form of sacrifice—a *yagna*. He explains, 'To give away the most prized possession, whom one has nurtured and cared for since birth, is considered as one of the greatest forms of giving. A parent blessed with a daughter achieves salvation if they can perform this yagna.'

Maa, an ardent believer of the Holy Scriptures, had read this passage when she was young, and the words remained etched in her subconscious ever since. Now, her wish was about to be realized, and soon she would perform this much-awaited yagna.

My elder brother, a liver surgeon

Best Friends...For Life!

The most commonly used words:
'Friend', 'best friend'.
Are you my friend?
Will you be my friend?
I wish to be your best friend...
Am I not your bestie?

Do we need to do anything to be that
For someone?
Do we really need to try,
Or can we simply be our own, real selves?

Many thoughts churn within,
Many images whirl before me.
We label ideologies,
We assign name tags.
Do you think anything of this
Is required? If yes, then they are not a friend!

Here, in my heart,
I define a friend as one who loves;
A lover who loves for love alone;
A friend for life!
A magical pull towards another,
Where, in time, the 'other' dissolves,
Becoming a natural extension

Of the one within.
That is the connect
To the essence of the word: Friend.

A friend is one
With whom we are transparent,
Who will never exploit the vulnerable side
Of the other, and be true come what may!

A friend becomes a true friend
When their tears bring tears to our eyes,
When their smile blooms a smile within us too!
It's not a commonly used word—*Best Friend*;
For it takes time, trust and love
To enter this sacred space!

Chapter 11

His Ways Are His Ways

With our maturity, we can only act to a certain extent. But when we surrender to His will and His ways, we witness magic unfolding for us at every moment!

Maa had surrendered herself entirely to her Krishna. She knew her God would always give her the best, and the universe conspired to bless her with the perfect groom for me. Being the only daughter and the most pampered, I had my own whims and fancies. As I mentioned earlier, I was already married to Krishna in my mind, just like Saint Meera Bai, whose story Maa had narrated to me countless times in my childhood, and I had no desire to marry anyone else.

But His ways are His ways, and we can never question them. We can only accept them with gratitude and grace.

Every move of God is divine, intricately and beautifully planned for each of us. He had a plan for me and for my mother's dream to be fulfilled.

There was a religious discourse on the Bhagavad Gita by a revered soul. During the event, my now husband, Parashar, walked up to the stage holding an idol of baby Lord Krishna. It was part of the ritual to place the idol in front of the holy scripture before commencing the talk. Parashar's father, being well acquainted with the revered soul, had requested Parashar to perform this honour.

Who could have known, except the Almighty, that on this very day, as I attended the discourse, I would see Parashar walking with the idol and give away my heart to him! Krishna had been my soulmate from childhood, and God blessed me with His form in Parashar.

When Professor Prema Pandurang (the revered saint) suggested to Maa that Parashar would be a suitable match for me, I immediately agreed. Through the discourse, Krishna had sent His form to me as my husband; how could I not surrender to His will?

Maa had played her part; she had introduced me to Narayana at an early age, and He flowed through her to bring abundance into mine. Miracles kept unfolding in my life through Maa's presence and guidance, and through my connection with God.

His ways are His ways, is what I always feel.

We must flow with His flow and surrender entirely to Him. When we do, He blesses us with more than we could ever expect or desire.

The day I saw Parashar walk up to the stage with the idol, something extraordinary happened. My gold chain, which had a heart-shaped pendant, fell on the stage as I went to receive the prasad. When people looked for its owner, it was found to be mine.

Miracles can never be explained, and this was no less than a miracle.

It was God's divine plan and a clear indication to me that Parashar was my destined husband. Krishna had sent him to guide me in my spiritual journey, even within the material world of marriage.

Whatever Maa dreamt for me manifested perfectly. She was, and remains, a powerful magnet of everything good, showing us that we can attract goodness by living life with maturity and spiritual alignment.

As Revered Mahātria says, 'The intent of the parent truly matters; all the forces of the universe especially bow down to the purest intent of a mother's heart.'

Dad managed to return just in time to meet Parashar. He had been in Vrindavan when the proposal was presented and rushed back to Kolkata to see the man chosen for his only daughter and give his consent.

Everything unfolded according to the divine plan and soon Parashar and I were married in the esteemed presence of Professor Prema Pandurang.

I saw Maa embodying the principle of *akrishtata*—her thoughts, words and actions were perfectly in sync, enabling the best outcomes for each one of us. Akrishtata teaches us that we attract what we think.

With the five of us married, Maa's major responsibilities were fulfilled. She gracefully stepped into her next role, ever prepared to embrace the new chapters of her life with love and wisdom.

The beginning of the most awaited chapter of my life

Life in a Cocoon

We have all lived in a cocoon,
The cocoon of our mother's womb.
Humans that we are,
This is the only way to take birth—
From a cocoon.

Then why do we lament,
Why wreathe in pain,
Why distress others,
Why create agony,
When we are souls of bliss!

The warmth in the womb,
The comfort within a shield,
The security we feel,
Inside that sacred place,
Hidden and protected from all—

This feeling is so easy to carry on
While we live in this earthly realm.
Which we call it our very own.
Yet in truth, nothing is our own
Except our thoughts and words.

Hence, these must be cocooned
As long as we are carried forth.

If we can stay pure for nine months within,
Why not hold that state henceforth,
With our intentions crystal clear!

In a shrouded mind, God does not dwell,
In a pretentious heart, God moves away.
So let us cocoon our Being—
To ignite, to uplift mankind,
To release the sorrow within.

That is cocooning of the soul
For its journey ahead.
Life will unfold as a flow and act we must
Rightfully, with alignment, to move
In harmony, in togetherness!

The mother's womb is a cocoon;
It cocoons not just our form
But our very thoughts and words.
It is not only for the newborn we rejoice—
We rejoice for rejoicing in itself;

For lifting our consciousness,
To a higher plane to uplift others
As a lofty tree offers shade
Our lofty thoughts elevates all
In doing so we live life to its HILT!

PART 2

BECOMING A MOTHER

In this section, I have shared my transformative experiences in fine-tuning the 'BEING' within me. This journey involved adapting to new environments, mastering the art of balancing work and home life, and immersing myself in the depths of respecting children through an integrated Montessori education course.

It is through these mindful efforts—nurturing the right thoughts, feelings and emotions towards children, and looking at them as independent beings—that I found myself blessed with the miracle of conception—the extraordinary gift of becoming a mother.

These 11 chapters unveil the sacred journey of nine months, divided into three trimesters of Deliberation, Liberation and Celebration.

I feel it is a must-read for mothers, mothers-to-be and even those who are scared of embracing motherhood; it is for anyone who wishes to marvel at the divine privilege of carrying another life within—an honour bestowed only upon women!

At its heart, this journey is one of celebration—of the profound connection with the spiritual embryo that grows within the sanctity of the womb!

Chapter 1

Have the Right Sangha

I had just gotten married, and life with Parashar was unfolding with its own exciting twists and turns. As an aspirational woman at heart, I carried a deep desire to become independent, achieve greatness and carve a unique identity for myself. Growing up in a household with four brothers, I often saw myself as one of them—eager to match their ambitions and drive.

In 1994, societal norms were quite different. Most girls in our community got married at 18, some even earlier. I, however, broke the mould and became the first daughter of the reputed Kanoria family in Kolkata to complete my graduation—a significant milestone for a girl from a conservative family like ours. I went against the wishes of my parents, who wanted me to marry right after completing school. I owe this achievement to the unwavering support of my brother Sanjeev, who convinced Dad to let me pursue my dreams and not follow the set norms.

Looking back, I resonate deeply with the words of Revered Mahātria: 'The beliefs you hold at the beginning of the journey define the journey.' I held firmly to the belief that I would complete my graduation, and life conspired to make it happen. I was married into an open-minded family, which allowed me to spread my wings and fly into the unknown.

Marriage, for me, was nothing short of a miracle. It wasn't just a union but a divine blessing, opening doors to a new chapter of my life. I was fortunate to find a partner in Parashar, who not only supported my aspirations but also shared a deep spiritual alignment with me. He became my companion in going deeper into my quest for divine consciousness.

As I settled into married life, my uncle-in-law became a pivotal influence. He encouraged all of us, including my eldest co-sister (a doctorate in science), to do something that added value to our lives and to that of others. His words propelled me into action, inspiring me to dream big for myself.

This was the moment when life conspired to bring me a serendipitous opportunity. A close school friend, Aditi, reached out and suggested I explore a Montessori course as I loved being with children. At the same time, she decided to pursue a career in fashion design at the National Institute of Fashion Technology (NIFT).

At that point, I had no idea what Montessori education entailed. Little did I know that this philosophy would become the cornerstone of my life, profoundly shaping not only my journey but also the lives of countless parents and children. I feel extreme gratitude towards her for being the right *sangha* (companion) when I required one.

In 1996, both of us embarked on our life-changing paths. I enrolled in the Montessori Diploma Training Course offered by the Indian Montessori Centre, Kolkata (an affiliate of the London Montessori Centre). Meanwhile, Aditi was among the very few students who gained direct admission to NIFT, one of India's most prestigious institutions, where chances of entry were unbelievably difficult.

It was no coincidence. Aditi and I had anchored ourselves in the belief of doing something meaningful in life—not just for personal gain but for a greater purpose.

A verse from the Bhagavad Gita, which I read as a daily ritual, still resonates deeply: 'One has to do seva as well as sadhana.' Neglecting one for the other creates disharmony. Even an ascetic must work.

These words became my guiding light. Through Montessori, I began to understand children at a deeper level. This understanding marked the beginning of one of the most enriching journeys of my life: being a mother.

Chapter 2

Montessori and Its Implications

Having grown up in a big joint family, surrounded by cousins, nieces, nephews, aunts and sisters-in-law, life after marriage felt starkly different. Transitioning to a nuclear family with just my husband, his parents and younger sister left me feeling lonely, and I missed having people around me. The decision to pursue Montessori training, in hindsight, was a blessing in disguise.

I consider myself fortunate to have married into a family that cherished aspirations, treating their daughters and daughter-in-law alike. Their support gave me the freedom to nurture my dreams and walk the path of purpose.

In June 1996, I began a journey of profound learning at the Indian Montessori Centre. The very first day of class transformed me completely as an individual. I vividly recall one teaching that resonated deeply: 'Come down to the level of the child and the world will look beautiful; from there, you will be able to relate to the child very easily.'

This was my lesson for a lifetime. It changed every aspect of who I was and how I viewed the world. From then on, my life took a turn, making it a core part of my identity. I have witnessed how life becomes beautiful when I see it from a child's perspective. Children never judge, and their emotions are genuine and immediate.

As I immersed myself in the Montessori method, my understanding of child psychology and concepts like the spiritual embryo deepened. The course not only transformed my perspective but also changed my interactions with children.

When we consistently reinforce positive emotions, we create a pattern in the child's mind. With an abundance of affirmations, the child is likely to hold on to positive feelings. Through this education, I noticed a significant shift within myself—I became incredibly tender towards children.

Earlier, I would scold my nieces or nephews to complete their meals or finish their homework. After the training, I no longer got angry at them. Instead, I would sit down with them, speak in their language, thereby developing the art of interacting with children. And lo! This approach worked like magic.

The Montessori method emphasizes repetition as a tool for mastery. Children instinctively repeat activities till they reach a point of satisfaction, after which they naturally move on to the next activity. This process not only instils consistency and excellence but also nurtures their ability to make independent choices from a young age.

There is a significant difference between a child who has undergone Montessori learning and one who has not. This philosophy continues to intrigue me, often leaving me overwhelmed with awe and gratitude. It became evident to me that my life had a purpose—to dedicate myself to the well-being of children and to guide parents in understanding their child through the child's perspective.

Paulo Coelho's words in *The Alchemist* resonate deeply with me: 'And, when you want something, all the universe conspires in helping you achieve it.'

The revelation of the spiritual embryo fills me with wonder every time I think about it. How marvellous it is that the infinite Creator designs each life with such precision and intricacy! This understanding instils a profound sense of gratitude and indebtedness for this human birth. I bow in reverence to all the forces that conspired to create me.

I often reflect on my existence as an extraordinary gift—a testament to God's grace and my mother's unwavering penance to have a daughter. I feel my life is a canvas painted with divine intention, and all I need to do is live it to the fullest, with extreme gratitude and purpose.

Montessori materials arranged and displayed

Something Is Happening within Me

Sometimes, we do not realize—
Life keeps going on in a particular pattern.
We feel a kind of boredom setting in
We feel enough is enough,
We feel like taking a break;

But to our surprise, the break
Leads to a breakthrough,
Calling out to us, 'Hey! What's next?'

I too was flowing through life—
Waking, working, praying, planning,
Holding on with grit and determination,
With renewed excitement and enthusiasm
That something would definitely come my way.

But life told me, 'Hey!
In the way itself, there is a way.
Why don't you figure it out?'

I was lost in some imaginary world,
Dreaming—or so I thought.
To my surprise, it was not a dream,
It was very much real;
As real as it can be.

I touched myself,
And marvelled: 'Wow! I can feel!
Yes, I can truly feel!'

Years ago, I had met Dr A.P.J. Kalam.
He taught me to dream—
To dream of a better world,
To dream of giving my best,
To dream with genuine desires
To manifest a brighter reality.

He taught me to dream beyond limits,
To break free of beliefs that confine.
To dream of becoming a better me.

Ever since, I have plunged into this realm,
Dreaming to be touched by God one day,
Dreaming to touch infinite lives,
Dreaming to be one among many,
To release attachments to materialism,
And direct my attachment towards the Divine.

I know when I turn to God,
He draws me closer,
To reveal Himself within.

In dreaming, I let go.
Let go of the material self,
Dropping expectations for all results.
Loving for love itself,
Never seeking to be loved in return.

Giving for the joy of giving,
Not longing to receive.

And as I let go,
Something happens within me!

A voice speaks softly,
Whispering silently yet resounding loud.
A paradox of stillness and noise,
Yet in this paradox is pure joy!
Joy in bringing happiness to others,
Joy in loving and giving selflessly.

In these moments, I feel beautiful.
I realize it is divinity to embrace beauty,
To rejoice in the success of others.
In truth, there is no *other;*
We are all but One!

In this Oneness, I feel God.
In this Oneness, I experience Life.

Through it all,
I feel a surge within—
An unstoppable gush of love,
Of bliss, of unshakable poise.
I feel alive. I feel whole.
I feel... *Something is happening within me!*

Chapter 3

The Montessorian Way

'With God in my team, everything is possible!'

The Montessori course was a demanding journey. I decided to take a year-long sabbatical from all external distractions to be able to give my best in this transformational process. I believed wholeheartedly it was possible because I had God at my side. Being with children is akin to being with God, and when you dedicate yourself to His work, He becomes your foremost assistant!

Each day I left home at 8.15 a.m. and returned by 2 p.m. My parents' home was close to the institute, and I often longed to visit my family on the way back. However, I had much to study at home, and every moment was extremely valuable. My routine was meticulously planned: reach home, have a quick lunch, take a half-hour nap and dedicate the afternoon and evening—from 3 p.m. to 8 p.m.—to studies and coursework.

By 8.30 p.m., Parashar would return home, and I reserved the rest of the evening for dinner and spending time together. I was so much in the flow of things that any deviation from this schedule felt disruptive—as though it would hamper my progress as a Montessori student and my duties as a wife.

As a married woman, I recognized the multiple obligations that came with the role. I was fortunate to have a mother-in-law who, as today's generation would call her 'cool', ensured I had the freedom to pursue my aspirations. I did not have to do any household chores or cook; she was happy taking care of those with the help of domestic assistants.

This freedom allowed me to give my best to the Montessori course, which was getting more interesting day by day. We started working on practical subjects and gained hands-on experience with the Montessori materials, which was one of the most gratifying aspects of my learning. Every moment, from the way we entered the classroom to the way we departed, was a lesson.

We were taught to give attention to every detail in seemingly mundane tasks—leaving footwear outside the door properly, writing neatly in notebooks and even folding letters to fit envelopes perfectly. These basic things are not usually taught in traditional schools. These small practices might seem trivial, but once embedded early, they form a strong impression in the subconscious mind of the child. With this solid foundation, children could aspire to achieve the unthinkable one day, even surpassing their own expectations!

The Montessori philosophy emphasizes that children learn more from seeing than hearing. When raised in an environment where adults model the right values, children naturally internalize these values and live accordingly.

The course was preparing me for life. Coming from a family where my parents were already role models, the Montessori principles enriched my growth further. Learning about child psychology, the spiritual embryo and adopting the disciplines imparted by the course cultivated greater peace, humility and maturity within me, aligning me with life's flow.

As the months progressed, the course became more intense. Submissions, assignments and practical learning kept us fully engaged. After completing the first term, we had to go for teaching practice. Each student was assigned to a nearby Montessori school for a month, where we were to assist the head Montessori guides. Each day, we documented our activities and observations, compiling detailed reports for submission. We repeated this practice for another month towards the end of the diploma degree; it provided us with two months of invaluable hands-on experience with children in a Montessori environment.

I thoroughly enjoyed my interactions with children as a Montessori teacher, and it was during this period that I discovered my *swadharma*—my true purpose. Being with children energized me and filled me with boundless joy. Hours would pass unnoticed as I immersed myself in their world, which continues for me. A harsh word from anyone towards a child takes me into an introverted state, making me feel more accountable for bringing about transformation in all caregivers.

The world of children

Chapter 4

Temporary Imbalances

To achieve a goal bigger than myself, I had to embrace temporary imbalances in life. Parashar has a vast friend circle, but I chose to withdraw from social commitments and focus entirely on the Montessori programme. The one-year diploma course was intense, delving deeply into child development and demanding immense time and attention. To let this transformation manifest completely, I accepted these imbalances, not as disruptions but as stepping stones.

Tapping into my swadharma of fostering the holistic development of children required unwavering dedication. Rather than unsettling me, these imbalances strengthened my resolve and prepared me to pursue my passion wholeheartedly. I have learnt that temporary imbalances often pave the way for peak performance in one sphere of life, enabling growth in unimaginable ways.

As I mentioned earlier, the course grew increasingly demanding as we progressed; submissions of projects, essays and thesis work became regular tasks. The primary subjects we studied were child development, child psychology, teaching practices, sociology, classroom management and classroom techniques—all requiring rigorous research and thoughtful writing.

In 1996, the internet was not a common household staple, so most of my research took place in libraries. Dad's office was very close to our house and had an extensive library with books spanning various subjects. I would head there early in the mornings, immersing myself in reading, reflecting and writing.

To my surprise, my papers and essays received distinctions, and the teachers even recommended them as reference materials for other students. I was pleasantly taken aback, yet very inspired. Writing had never been my forte. Throughout school, I had struggled with languages—be it Hindi or English. I loved mathematics and had always envisioned myself as a businesswoman or a chartered accountant like my brother. However, the Montessori course led to a profound awakening in me. Words began to flow naturally, as if my inner self had found its voice.

Early morning writing sessions at Dad's office, classes at the institute, teaching practices at the Montessori house and submissions of project work occupied nearly all my time. Yet I found time for my hobbies—reading, listening to music and watching movies with my husband at the theatres. Television, however, was strictly off-limits at home.

I looked forward to Saturdays when I would spend the day with my parents and my nieces and nephews. Even though I carried my coursework with me, being with family, especially the little ones, rejuvenated me. Whenever I went there, they would snuggle with me; they were the initial spark that ignited my passion for understanding child psychology and dedicating my life to working with children.

Life went on and amidst the hectic schedule, I did not have the time to socialize with friends and extended family. Surprisingly, I never felt I was missing out. My life, despite its temporary imbalances, felt fulfilling—rich with focus, passion and determination to excel.

What I realized was that life has its own way of recalibrating.

I recall the profound words of my beloved Mahātria: 'Less will make it long; more will make it short.'

The time I spent with Parashar, though limited, became more meaningful. We cherished our moments together even more and looked forward to them. The scarcity of time made every shared moment precious.

The temporary imbalances that demanded time, concentration and excellence in one sphere of my life brought balance and depth to the others. With unflinching faith and a grateful heart, I moved forward happily in this journey, knowing that these sacrifices were shaping me for something greater.

The joy of working with Montessori materials

Dualities of Nature

There is a deep desire to become one—
One with the all-encompassing One!
One with the other, as we all are apart,
Yet truly, we all are one when we realize oneness,

To realize oneness takes years,
As we are all born of bone and flesh.
To transcend bodily tendencies,
To rise beyond the mind and heart
Is what we strive for...
Oneness makes us go deep within,
Accept ourselves as we are,
And connect with the One within.

In knowing ourselves, we know the other—
Not through effort, but through grace.
Dualities dissolve, opposites fade...
Or so it seems, to me!

In reality, dualities never cease,
They are threads of nature's weave.
This cosmos, created by a Higher Force,
An Energy that governs us, unfolds our oneness!

The masculine and feminine energies,
The cycle of day and night,
The seasons that come and go—
Reflects to us we are transient too, and one day,

We too shall pass; but till we exist,
What is our nature that defines us?
Why do we all crave to become one?
One with the other who attracts us,
A magnetic pull, ignited by chemical reactions—
Life's sacred urge to procreate,
To ensure the race continues,
To create, to leave legacies…

In this Oneness,
We experience *shunya*—an emptiness within
Which feels more complete.
Ecstasy and bliss overpowers the within—
Prem Sat Chit Anand becomes our very state,
A union of existence, consciousness and bliss.

Chapter 5

One without a Second

While my life was at its peak with studies and projects, I always looked forward to spending quality time with Parashar. We had been married for two years by 1996, and Parashar always respected my aspirations to pursue something beyond the conventional role of a homemaker. I made sure to complete my studies before he returned from work so that we could have uninterrupted time together. These moments created a sense of completeness amidst our busy schedule, deepening our bond.

Life moved along with enthusiasm and excitement, and everything seemed to fall into place effortlessly. There was a lightness in everything that I did, as it came from a place of deep passion and commitment.

As Revered Mahātria says, 'Doing that which energizes you is your swadharma.' Deep down, I knew I had found mine.

Thanks to my regimented father, I had developed the habit of waking up early—a discipline ingrained since my school days. Dad had always prioritized health, insisting that we engage in physical activities to build our resilience. We were literally dragged from bed at early hours in the morning to practise yoga with him. He ensured to take us for swimming, badminton or lawn tennis at a club on weekdays and for extended hours during the weekend.

He firmly believed in the philosophy of Swami Vivekananda: 'Nerves of steel, muscles of iron and minds like thunderbolt'

For Dad, physical fitness was not just a necessity—it was a

foundation for emotional harmony as well as mental vigilance.

With my mother's passion for dancing and me being a girl, Maa made me learn Kathak, a classical dance form, from the age of five. All these made me physically strong to take on any challenges in life. These early experiences instilled discipline, strength and grace—traits that helped me juggle my studies, manage the household and spend meaningful time with Parashar.

After dinner, Parashar and I would retire to our room. In our small family of five, there was not much to do after dinner except be with each other or watch television. Sometimes Parashar would join his friends for short drives or coffee; I joined him occasionally. I was just happy being with him as spending time together mattered the most to me. His charisma and intelligence always shone in every interaction, and his friends looked up to him for his impressive communication skills and professional expertise as a chartered accountant.

Despite my love for him, I was a meek and shy person, especially when it came to physical intimacy. I always looked to him to take the lead, but all that truly mattered to me was to make him feel loved.

As Revered Mahātria says, 'What you serve, you get attached to.' In serving, we only think of the other, and through seva, love is deepened.

My mother had once shared a shloka from the Bhagavad Gita with me, which explained that the seed is the father and the womb is Mother Nature. Like Mother Earth, women possess an innate ability to nurture, adapt and bear all that life brings, while the seed represents the father's potential to procreate. Both have to work in harmony and unison to create a life, blessed with the grace and presence of God.

As these thoughts churned within my mind, heart and soul, I found myself surrendering completely to the moment and to this beautiful concept of the union of male and female energies. In this sacred union of love, passion and togetherness, the divine force was shaping a new life—signalling a journey that would just begin.

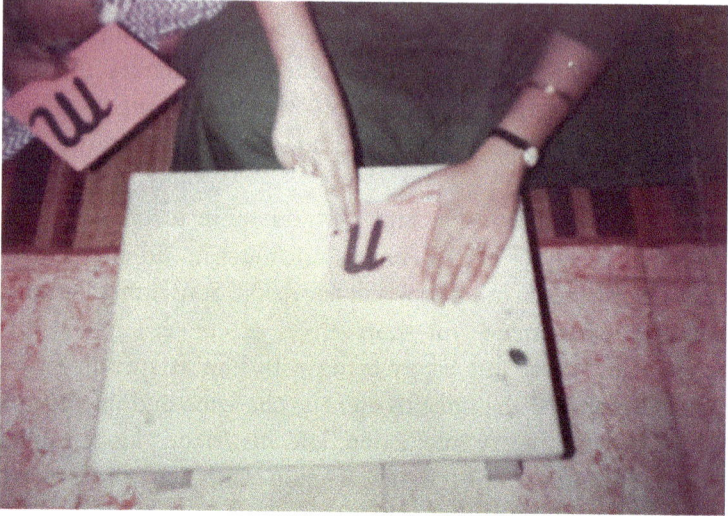

Learning to read and write through tracing

Chapter 6

Happy News

The much-awaited news, which the families had been longing to hear, was finally ready to be shared. For me, it felt almost surreal. I did not even realize when it happened; all I knew was how I had chanted the shloka silently during those special moments.

Perhaps that's how it is meant to be—when we do not overthink, everything unfolds according to God's divine plan, which is always the best that could happen! Parashar was overjoyed when I shared the news with him and embraced me in his quiet, loving manner. For the family, it was a blessing they had been eagerly waiting for.

To be frank, I felt like I was living in another dimension, immersed in a plethora of thoughts—not for myself, but for children. I had no clue about many things, but with this beautiful moment transpiring in my life, I realized I had to hasten my process of learning.

I was in complete AWE (capitalized to emphasize the depth of my emotions) of the divine notion of conception. The sacred words from the Bhagavad Gita permeated every cell of my very being. My heart and soul seemed to be profoundly connected with God. The term 'spiritual embryo', as used by Dr Maria Montessori to describe the emerging life, reverberated within me.

In this moment, I felt an 'AHA'—a profound sense of wonderment! I closed my eyes and thanked God for blessing me with His divine presence within me—now in the form of a new life. My journey as a mother—a life within a life—began from that very moment.

The teachings from my Montessori course stirred within me. I gently touched my tummy, where my baby had just begun to make their home, and smiled…

I knew I would play my part well in nurturing this little life. The detailed studies from my course about the womb and the child's agony during the dark, mysterious period of gestation resonated deeply.

I understood that as a mother-to-be with knowledge about the spiritual embryo, it was my responsibility to channel my energy in the right direction. It was essential to nurture the emotional, intellectual, spiritual and psychological development of the child within me. For that, I needed to maintain my own alignment—physically, mentally and spiritually. A spiritually rooted mother, I believed, would contribute effectively to the growth of a spiritual embryo.

For a few moments, it felt as though the world around me had paused. Overwhelmed by the weight of this responsibility, I wondered if I would be able to do justice to the life developing within me. A wave of positive emotions surged through me, and I felt jolted yet inspired.

In that moment of epiphany, Dr Maria Montessori's words popped up in my mind: 'We should regard this secret effort of the child as something sacred. We should welcome its arduous manifestations, since it is in this creative period that an individual's future personality is determined.'

The child within me, this spiritual embryo, would embark on a secret journey, shaped by my actions and energy. I realized that this period was the most sacred one for me—one where my actions over the next nine months would profoundly influence the development and future personality of this spiritual being. All this would happen only if I engaged in the right actions as there is a direct correlation between actions and feelings.

I accepted this truth gracefully, letting it seep into every part of my being. Feeling a sense of peace, bliss and immense gratitude, I opened my eyes.

The first call I made was to my mother as I knew she would be delighted and bless me. She has been my guiding light, my inspiration and continues to show me the right way to live with grace and wisdom.

I reflected on the sacred sequence of life's most significant forces:

Matha, Pitha, Guru, Deivam (Mother, Father, Teacher, God)— everything in life happens in perfect synchronization with these four pillars.

For the moment, it was time to bask in the joy of the happy news making its way into the hearts of everyone who loved and cherished me.

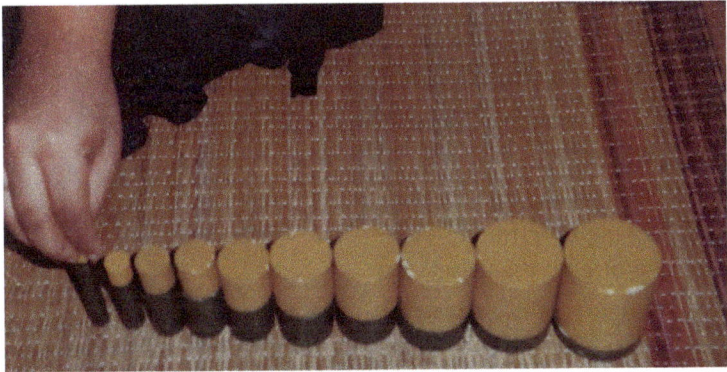

Developing fine motor skills

Conceived—Really!

Ahaa! Life, I wonder—
How can it bear one within,
One's own self—how is it possible?

Ahaa! Life, I wonder—What is not possible,
When God decides to manifest within?
In someone, when love and passion unite—
A creation born out of giving and receiving.

Ahaa! Life, I wonder—When does this happen?
When we let
the other go ahead,
And give—simply for
The sake of giving and serving.

Ahaa! Life, I wonder—Why has God made this so divine?
When there is selflessness,
When there is true love for the other—
It just happens, beyond thought or reason.

Ahaa! Life, I wonder—Where is God not?
In everything that has life—He is!
In that which holds no life—He is not!
He is a formless presence in all forms.

Ahaa! Life, I wonder—Which form does He come in?
He comes in One who is love,
He abides in One who gives love—
Hence, I conceived, really!

Aha! Life, I wonder—How can it bear one within,
One's own self—how is it possible!
It happened to me,
It can happen to all those who love!

Chapter 7

The First Three Months

The first three months of pregnancy are the formative months when the baby begins to take shape. This is a crucial period, particularly for the mother's physical health, and she needs utmost care during this time. Many women are advised to rest by their doctors, as the body adjusts to housing a new life within. These early months are often accompanied by vomiting and nausea.

For me, the first trimester was a time of significant difficulty. Severe nausea and vomiting plagued me, and my gynaecologist recommended a few tests that revealed my hormone levels were on the lower side. To address this, I had to receive weekly injections to stabilize my condition. My doctor is one of the most sought-after gynaecologists in Kolkata, and to get an appointment with him was fairly difficult. My brothers knew him personally, and he took care of me with the affection of a father rather than just a doctor.

He would visit me at home as he did not want me to travel in the car for the first three months. His visits were a delightful sight—my mother-in-law, a petite woman, would often scurry after him, fretting over me and the baby, while he, a towering figure, reassured her.

'Maa ji,' he would say, looking straight into her eyes, 'Why do you worry so much when I am there? Your daughter-in-law will give birth to a son like Amitabh Bachchan. Then you can treat me to a feast at Taj Bengal!'

Her quiet smile in response, coupled with his swift yet thorough check-ups, brought a sense of calm and amusement to our household. He was like an express train—speeding in, ensuring everything was fine, and rushing back to his clinic.

This phase was also significant academically, as I was nearing the end of my Montessori Diploma Course. Assignments and projects loomed large, with my final examinations scheduled for June. The practical exams were to be assessed by examiners from London, while the theory papers were to be evaluated by different examiners in the UK. It was an important period and I wanted to do my best, but my physical health was not always favouring me as I was nurturing a life within.

Despite my physical struggles, I embraced the changes with a pleasant demeanour, rooted in my awe of the concept of motherhood. I was determined to give my best, knowing that nurturing children and mastering the art of being with them was akin to doing God's work. When we dedicate ourselves to His work, He takes care of the rest! My faith replaced all the question marks I had with exclamations to express my gratitude and joy.

I was blessed to have a family who supported and believed in what I was doing. Seeing my determination despite my fragile health, my mother-in-law, aunt-in-law and sister-in-law pitched in to help me complete my projects. This was 1996, a time without any access to the internet; the research work involved poring over books and flipping through magazines to gather necessary materials.

It was a true carpe diem moment—our family united, sitting together and working as one to help me complete my work that had now become theirs too. The memory of those final days of my Montessori course remains etched in my heart. I feel deeply grateful for every force that worked in my favour to get me through this last phase successfully with peace.

The next situation was the final exams. Would my doctor allow me to commute 30 minutes each way to the institute and back? Forgoing the exams meant waiting for an entire year to reattempt, with the next set of students. How would I do justice to the course if I took my exam a year later? With a newborn to care for, my attention would undoubtedly be divided, and the subjects I had studied for would no longer be fresh in my memory.

I had to persuade my doctor, and I did. I told him that he had to figure out a way so that I could travel on the days of the exams. Initially, he was not convinced as it meant risking two lives. After much persistence, he agreed—on one condition. A sonography would be performed to ensure the safety of both me and the baby. Only if the results were satisfactory would he permit the travel. Additionally, I would have to stay at my maternal home, which was close to the institute. This would make things easier for me and the little one.

The sonography reports came out perfect, and commuting to the institute was no longer a bar. The cherry on the cake was getting to stay with my mother during the days of the exams! Everything fell into place seamlessly—my exams, the support of my family and the presence of children who inspired me at every step. On the morning of the exam, as I prepared to leave for the institute, I closed my eyes and whispered a silent prayer: 'Thank you, God, my beloved, my friend. Thank you for loving me so much. Thank you for blessing me with an abundance of love in every aspect of life. Thank you doesn't feel enough, yet that is all I can offer as your child. THANK YOU!'

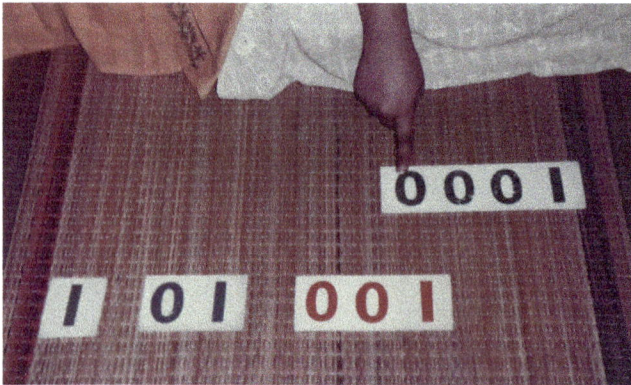

Learning numbers

Chapter 8

The Second Trimester

Even though my physical health wasn't at its peak, my mental and emotional health soared to unprecedented heights. The sheer joy and excitement of carrying a life within me eclipsed any physical discomfort I was experiencing.

As Revered Mahātria says, 'The mind of the man is the man. Man is the sum total of his subconscious mind than the conscious one. Whatever he decides to achieve, he is able to accomplish with the strength of the mind.'

I lived this truth daily. The deep sense of happiness and love that fuelled my mind, mentally energized me despite the intermittent discomforts of my physical state.

My final examination involved five theory papers, each on a different subject. Missing even one paper would mean disqualification. The exams were scheduled for two hours, but it often took me five hours to complete each one. The process was interrupted frequently by bouts of nausea and vomiting.

I am extremely grateful to my Montessori teacher, who sat by me while I was writing the exams. She encouraged me to keep writing and helped me eat something whenever I felt uneasy. She recognized the necessity of balancing mental focus with physical nourishment during this stage. While other students noticed the special attention I received, they refrained from questioning the situation, respecting the decisions of the senior-most teacher.

The Montessori philosophy had deeply inspired me, and my passion for the subject flowed naturally onto the exam papers.

Despite the difficulties, I completed all my exams within two days. With the submission of my projects and the end of the theory and practical exams, I felt a profound sense of relief. I could now dedicate the next six months to nurturing my physical, psychological, mental and emotional well-being, which was essential for the baby's development.

As I stepped into the second trimester, the nausea began to subside, and my focus shifted inwards. I devoted myself to connecting with God, aspiring to raise a spiritually aligned child. The teachings of the Montessori course were extremely fresh in my mind, which helped me to take care of the life within me. I viewed the baby as God's child, one who is eternally with Him!

My daily routine became more relaxed without the need to commute to the institute. I still woke up early and started attending a spiritual discourse from 8 a.m. to 9 a.m. This gave me a lot of spiritual strength to carry on the day vigilantly and be useful in some way or the other for the people around me. I started practising yoga and breathing exercises in the morning, and also walked for an hour in the evening to enhance my physical health.

Diet played an important part during this time and I concentrated on eating healthy food rather than indulging in delicacies, breaking the common myth of 'eating for two'. Instead, I ate mindfully, as much as my body required.

My intellectual and spiritual growth continued to flourish. The Montessori institute selected me as an examiner to correct papers for the current batch of students—a task that enriched my learning and inspired me to keep growing. I surrounded myself with uplifting company, immersed myself in enriching literature and ensured my emotions remained elevated.

I would visit my parents' home frequently, spending time with everyone, especially my nieces and nephews. I enjoyed infinite unforgettable moments with them, cherishing their company and the innocence they brought into my life. Evenings were spent enjoying quality time with Parashar, after he came back from his work. I would discuss my day with him, talk about my health and reflect on the spiritual insights I gained from the morning discourse.

By the fifth month, it was time for another sonography to check the baby's growth. The results were encouraging—everything was progressing well, thanks to the hormone injections that had balanced my parameters. I had not embraced the art of meditation yet, but my surroundings were always filled with bhajans and religious chants by Professor Prema Pandurang, whose blessings had graced our marriage and permeated our home.

Parashar was extremely caring and loving, making sure he always accompanied me to the doctor's. My tummy had started to show, and at times, I could feel my baby kicking. Whenever this happened, I would get very excited and, if Parashar was around, I would ask him to place his hands on my tummy. What a feeling it was—inexpressible!

There's a saying: 'A baby fills a place in your heart that you never knew was empty.' This sentiment perfectly captured my emotions. At this stage, I felt elevated in every sense—emotionally, mentally, physically, intellectually and spiritually.

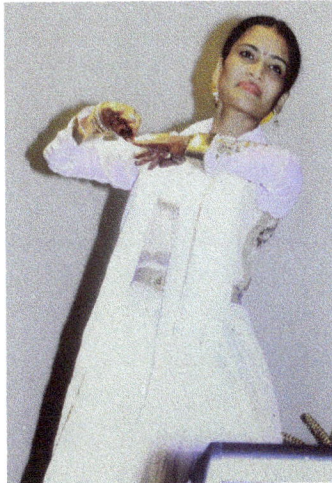

The joy of dancing

In My Womb

In my womb,
I experience God;
In my God,
I experience stillness;
In my stillness,
I experience peace;
In my peace,
I experience divinity.

Through divinity,
I experience faith;
In my Faith,
I experience bliss;
In my bliss,
I experience infinity;
In infinity,
I experience eternity.

From eternity,
I feel a flow;
In this flow,
I experience truth;
In truth,
I feel one with God;
In feeling one with God,
I feel one with all.

This, I realize,
Is God's love—
Infinite, eternal,
Inexpressible.
Without thoughts,
Flowing as a river—
Unblocked, inexhaustible,
Bearing a life,
As I feel in my womb.

Chapter 9

The Third Trimester

Life was moving in full swing, and I was enjoying every moment of my pregnancy. Even with occasional uneasiness at the physical level, the movement of another life within me filled me with a joy I had never experienced before. This unique experience gave me such profound happiness that I often found myself thinking, 'I would love to hold another life within me, again and again.'

I wished I could shout from the rooftops about the euphoria of this experience. But even if I couldn't then, it is never too late to share now. Perhaps my words will inspire someone to embrace the idea of motherhood. Fear of motherhood, sadly, has become a barrier for many young people today, deterring them from marriage and parenthood altogether. As you continue reading, I hope any anxieties about carrying another life within you will melt away.

◆

While waiting for my doctor's appointment, surrounded by other expectant mothers at various stages of pregnancy, I felt a deep connection with them. These nine months were not just about my baby's growth; these were also a journey for Parashar and me to grow as parents. As I sat there, eyes closed, I reflected on the past six months. Joy and sadness mingled within me—joy at the thought of holding my little one soon and sadness knowing that I would no longer feel the little kicks and playful movements within me.

In the midst of this reverie, I felt a gentle touch on my lap. I opened my eyes slowly, immediately recognizing the familiar warmth—it was none other than my dearest Parashar. His presence made me feel as though the entire world was by my side. Over the last six months, his tenderness and care had been unparalleled. In that moment, I silently resolved to go through this beautiful journey of pregnancy as many times as life allowed.

Soon the receptionist called out our name, and we were ushered into the sonography room. As I lay on the bed, my eyes scanned the computer screen where the tiny bundle of life moved within the limited space of my womb.

Tears trickled down my cheeks as my thoughts wandered to the Montessori chapter: 'The Spiritual Embryo'. It describes how a baby struggles within the womb to grow.

The baby longs to come out of the dark womb, which is a temple nurturing a new life. When a baby emerges after nine months, the first cry is often misunderstood—it is not sadness but relief and joy at being free. At the same time, it is a poignant paradox—the cry could also symbolize detachment from the mother, the source of life, or the daunting return to the material world.

Lost in these thoughts, I barely noticed when Parashar tapped me back to reality. The sonographer had turned up the monitor volume and asked us to close our eyes. What we heard next was unforgettable—the rhythmic beating of our baby's heart. The sound reverberated through me, freezing me in that moment of awe. Even now, as I write these words, the memory gives me goosebumps.

◆

By my seventh month, I was in excellent health. Walking, swimming, practising yog and pranayama, squatting, maintaining a healthy diet and having a sound sleep schedule kept me extremely fit and active. Towards the end of my seventh month, Parashar and I decided to take a short trip before the baby arrived. We wanted to spend as much time as we could with each other before we would become responsible for another life!

I left the choice of destination up to Parashar because I knew he would pick the best one. For me, being with him was what mattered the most; the location was secondary. I only wanted access to a swimming pool, as I had been swimming every day since the fifth month of my pregnancy and wanted to continue with this routine.

Somehow, my mind had tuned into the idea of giving birth in water, as I believed it would be the best experience. Visualizing the entire scene filled me with sheer excitement! I had read that the foetus in the last trimester is very sensitive to sounds. The baby becomes drawn to certain sounds and, upon birth, can recognize those heard while in the womb. I was particularly intrigued by the sound of water, the chirping of birds, the ringing of the temple bells, the sound of *aum* and the soundless yet divine aura of silence. I was determined to experience all of these.

Parashar booked tickets for us to visit Jaipur and Udaipur in Rajasthan during October, coinciding with the Durga Puja vacations in Kolkata. We spent a week in both cities, staying in excellent hotels, which elevated the experience. Yet the essence of our trip lay in the time we spent together. We talked, sat close, looked into each other's eyes and held hands as we walked slowly.

Parashar made sure that I took every step carefully, as he was also the creator of the life growing within me. I felt this was one of the best holidays we'd ever shared, and I cherish those days even now, as memories flash through my mind.

'When you feel that first little kick and hear a tiny heartbeat for the first time, you suddenly understand what it means to love someone more than your own life.'

That was exactly how we both felt—crazy in love with the tiny life I was carrying. Thanks to this journey, I became a mother. Ah, motherhood!

MANISHA LOHIA
DIRECTRESS

My pride and joy

Chapter 10

The Labour of Love

The three trimesters were the most beautiful and sacred phases of my life. I did everything a mother could do to nurture and deliver a spiritually aligned child. Nothing mattered more to me than the well-being of the growing life within me. Just as every mother gives her best in giving birth to a new life, I too was devoted to this divine responsibility.

Growing a little life inside you is no simple task. The morning sickness, the fluctuating hormones, the changes to the body and the sleepless nights can be overwhelming. Yet, when it gets too hard, just remember how powerful you really are. You are growing a life inside you, which is incredible.

But for mothers, this world would not exist.

By the third week of December, I was in my last trimester. My brother had come to visit us from London during the Christmas break, coinciding with Dad's birthday on the 31st. Surprisingly, I had not put on much weight except for a few kilos, and my stomach had barely protruded. I was quite comfortable with my body even though it had expanded in size. In fact, I rejoiced every time I noticed my tummy growing slightly bigger. The kicks of the little one were thrilling!

I found myself reflecting on the journey of the past eight months, which had gone by so smoothly and swiftly. It felt like a movie playing in my mind—the happy news, Parashar's gentle hug, the joys of the first trimester, the Montessori exams, the early morning religious gatherings, the healthcare regime and the time I spent with my parents, family and children. Life was unfolding beautifully, and I treasured every moment.

One of the most special experiences was my visits to the gynaecologist. Parashar would always accompany me, and I loved the sense of responsibility he showed towards the life we were bringing into the world. While I carried the baby within, he made the journey special with his love. Believe me, when you are in love, everything feels so effortless. That is the beauty of love!

The love I had for my baby kept me excited yet composed throughout the nine months. Nothing was on my mind other than the child growing within me. My thoughts, words and actions were always aligned with what I wanted my baby to feel, hear and experience. With Parashar by my side and God within me, these nine months felt like a joyful roller coaster ride with all its interesting bends and curves.

The most thrilling moment of this journey was when the sonographer rolled the scanner on my extended belly and pointed out the moving foetus on the screen. I was in awe and absolutely fascinated by this human life and its intricacies.

How fragile we were in reality, when created within our mother's womb; yet how bold we become, shaped by the thoughts and energy surrounding us from the very beginning.

My eyes would scan every part of the foetus, marvelling at the miracle forming within my body—a body gifted by my parents and God. In that moment, I connected deeply with Kahlil Gibran's profound words:

'Your children are not your children.
They are the sons and daughters of Life's longing for itself.
They come through you but not from you,
And though they are with you yet they belong not to you.

You may give them your love but not your thoughts,
For they have their own thoughts.
You may house their bodies but not their souls,
For their souls dwell in the house of tomorrow...'

Tears of joy, love, happiness and gratitude welled up in my eyes. I felt profoundly blessed, in every possible way to house the body of my baby but not the soul, and give my baby my love but not my thoughts—for the baby had come through me but not from me.

In that moment, I made a silent pledge. This life, which was coming through me, would grow to fulfil its fullest potential, soaring swiftly and far, like an arrow touching many lives.

The nine months of this sacred journey were nothing short of sadhana—my heartfelt devotion to God, as cells formed and a life grew within me. The time was fast approaching when I would finally hold this precious being in my hands and nurture them in the tangible form of a child!

Like a gardener, I would dedicate myself to nurturing this little seed, helping it sprout into a plant and, eventually, into a flowering tree, which would offer fruits and shade to many.

I was in complete awe of becoming a Maa—the most adorable angel! What I felt for my own mother, someone would soon feel for me.

The final month before delivery

The Spiritual Embryo

Behold folks! The spiritual embryo
Takes shape within a divine heart.
Hold yet a while, O pure being of mine—
It is in this holding that life creates!

It emerges with all its might,
Yet its power is not its own.
The might is that of the Infinite,
Bringing joy to all, fairly untold!

Behold folks! The spiritual embryo
Takes shape between two ecstatic hearts.
Hold yet a while, O pure being of love—
It is in this calmness that life is born!

Reflector true—your pulse is tuned to mine.
In a mother's womb, you take root,
A perfect symphony of grace and rhythm,
Ready to now part… Recorder—say!

Behold folks! It is the spiritual embryo,
Shaped tenderly within a cocoon.
No time to hold anymore as all is done,
It is in this parting that a new life begins!

Chapter 11

The Preparations

When we give birth to our baby, we also give birth to an incredible strength within us and a love that only comes with motherhood.

Everything was progressing smoothly, and by eight and a half months, euphoria filled the air as my due date—26 January—drew near. The thought of holding my little one in my arms overwhelmed me with joy. Throughout the last few months, I had done everything possible to prepare for a normal delivery. I wanted to go through the natural way of delivering rather than be operated on, even though I knew it came with immense pain. Yet, it is that very pain—coupled with unparalleled bliss—that truly defines motherhood.

I wanted to experience the profound moment of bringing a new life into this world—a moment that elevates a woman to the status of a mother. The pain of childbirth becomes a source of lifelong strength—a protective force that binds mother and child for eternity. The umbilical cord, though severed at birth, forms a cordless bond that transcends time.

At the end of December, my gynaecologist, Dr Pranab Dasgupta, suggested a scan to review the baby's condition. The sonographer followed the usual procedures, and once again, I found myself marvelling at the sight of my baby floating within me, connected by the cord of life. It was a bittersweet moment, as I realized this might be the last time that I would see my little one this way.

I wondered if I would feel this joy again in the future. Would I bear many more children or would this be the first and last? It was a question only God would be able to answer, for who was I to decide the birth of a child? Birth is a divine decision, best left in the hands of the Infinite.

The scan revealed that the baby was not growing as expected, and keeping him in the womb any longer would be unwise. A caesarean delivery was recommended—something I had never wanted, right from the beginning of my pregnancy. I had prepared myself for a natural birth, willing to embrace the physical and emotional demands it entailed. The idea of surgery felt foreign and disappointing at first, but life had its own plans.

I turned to my brother Sanjeev, a liver transplant surgeon, for advice. Since he was in India at that time, I asked him to meet my gynaecologist and discuss the possibility of a normal delivery. Whatever Sanjeev suggested, I was ready to follow.

He met my doctor to assess the situation and explained its intensity to me. He reassured me of my overall good health; my blood pressure was normal, my weight gain was adequate and I had taken excellent care of myself. The only drawback was that the child was no longer growing according to the gestation period. Waiting for a natural delivery could risk complications for both of us.

Sanjeev emphasized that surgery was the safest option. If the baby's weight was below average, the little one might need to be kept in an incubator for a few weeks. Hearing this, I was taken aback and questioned why. Almost immediately, I wondered: *Wow, this too must be part of God's plan!*

What if something went wrong during the normal delivery? Surgery would prevent complications. Although I would miss experiencing the labour pain I had prepared myself for, this was indeed the best decision for both the baby and me. I realized the present circumstances required a new perspective. I surrendered to the divine plan and told Sanjeev to proceed with whatever he felt was appropriate.

Parashar, as always, prioritized my well-being. For him, my health came first, followed by the baby's. He was deeply concerned, especially since I had not put on much weight during the pregnancy. While I had always hoped for a daughter (having always longed for a sister and cherishing the thought of a baby girl), Parashar's only wish was for a healthy child. Sex didn't matter to him.

I was excited yet slightly perturbed by the thought of not delivering naturally. Deep inside, I decided that if a normal delivery was not possible, I would still push myself to get out of bed soon after the surgery. I had heard stories about mothers struggling with post-surgery pain and remaining bedridden after caesarean births. But I resolved not to let that deter me. I affirmed to myself that I would muster all my strength and get up, even if it meant feeling massive pain.

This resolve would bring me as close as possible to experiencing a natural birth and provide the satisfaction of feeling the profound transformation of becoming a mother.

On 8 January 1998, I was admitted to Woodlands Nursing Home in Alipore, Kolkata. At 27, I was about to become a young mother. The nurses tried to make me comfortable, suggesting ways to reorganize my belongings so everything would be in place once the baby arrived. They were surprised to learn I was due the next day. My bump was so small that they thought I was only five months pregnant!

Later that evening, there was a knock on the door. My *satsang* friends had come to visit. Their words filled me with divine hope and faith: 'Manisha, everything will be fine. Do not see your child as weak or small. What you look at, you will manifest. The first glance of a mother shapes her child's destiny. Look at your baby as healthy and fit, and they will grow into that. The way we see, so it becomes.'

The next morning, these words echoed in my mind as the doctor took me to the operation theatre. Just before putting me under anaesthesia, I heard him whispering to me: 'Manisha, your dad wishes for the baby to be born before

12 p.m. Can you see the time now? It is 11.50 a.m. Your little one will arrive before noon. When you wake up, you will see two beautiful eyes trying to look at you.'

These were the last words I heard before drifting into another world!

PATIENT : MRS M LOHIA   AGE : 26 YEARS
                                          DATE : 05 01 98

OBSTETRICAL SONOGRAM
LMP   :19th April'97
Indication:Fetal growth study

A singleton viable **Small for Date** fetus in cephalic presentation. Head is high-up.**!!**

Heart rate is 142B/min....regular.

Cervix is tubular with no effacement.

Liquor amnii is **less** for the period.
There are a few small fluid pockets.

Placenta is posterior and maturity is **Term-type** i.e.......Fall-out zones: +
                                          ....Micro-calcifications: + + .

GESTATIONAL PARAMETERS

B P D	...... 91 mm	Gestational age	...... 33.4 weeks...SFD
Femur	...... 66 mm	Menstrual age	...... 37.2 weeks
T B D	...... 88 mm	Estimated weight	...... 2458 gms(approx)
Abd circumf	...... 287 mm		

Fetal head is normal.

Accepting God's Plan

Last scan of little Ved inside me

Cordless Connection

Where darkness is seen as light,
Where pain masquerades as happiness,
Where long night are mistaken for health—It is here a soul is
born, and time slips away
Into oblivion, till a newborn's cry awakens all to life!

It is this cordless connection I speak of,
Born of love, where the *jivatma* unites
With the *paramatma* to fulfil life's longing
For itself—a purpose destined by Brahman.
Yet, why do we lose it as this cord is severed?

The umbilical cord must disconnect the soul
To give it life, to let it thrive by itself.
But in doing so, why do we lose the eternal cord—
with the one that binds us to God as long as we live?
And when we are no more, the cord slips away too.

Should we not retain this cordless connect eternally?
It binds us to our primal force within
And, in turn, to the Eternal Force pervading all.
I often pity those who fail to realize this sacred bond,
But then I wonder—what is there to pity?

Should I not be the reformer to make this truth unfold
Rather than waste my time in pitying?
I see the birds soaring high, the butterflies fluttering,
As humans, we too must keep flying and striving,
Rising higher than the limitless sky with our thoughts!

Pure thoughts will make any force bow down,
As life paves the way for a resolute soul.
The stronger this cordless connection,
The more effortlessly life unfolds—
All we must do is love and hold on!

Holding long enough is the key,
Holding on to the Infinite storehouse of Energy!
To fill all lives with purity, selflessness and love.
In a pure heart, God resides, and effort becomes effortless,
And the cordless connection then sets its pace right.

PART 3

BEING A MOTHER

This is the most sacred section as I finally became a mother, having nurtured a life within me for nine months. The words I have penned in this section come from my deepest experiences, echoing the universal journey that every mother undertakes after giving birth.

What I have learnt through these experiences is what I now wish to share with my readers—especially those who are mothers or those who soon desire to tread this path.

It is often assumed that once the baby is delivered, everything will naturally fall into place. We tend to focus primarily on the nine months of pregnancy, believing that the real work ends there. While these nine months create and shape the growing embryo within, the journey of nurturing doesn't stop at birth; the responsibility grows as we begin tuning our children to the rhythms of life through right thoughts, words and actions.

In this section of the book, I share how the inner being evolves, becoming more patient, accepting, loving, peaceful and joyful. These are qualities every mother aspires to embody, and it's through this beautiful transformation that we too grow into our most authentic selves.

Through the discovery of the child, we discover a new version of ourselves—one that I wish to share with my readers here!

Chapter 1

Discovery of a New Me

After delivering my little one, it felt as though I was born again. The most beautiful thing about pregnancy is that you are not just creating a child but also creating a mother. And here I was—a mother created in this sacred process!

As the nurses wheeled me out of the operation theatre, I heard a voice calling out to me, 'Didi, congratulations! You have given birth to a baby boy.'

It was Sangita Bhabhi, who had been waiting for the baby's arrival before heading off to London. She had been outside the theatre, brimming with excitement to share the happy news with me. Everyone in the family was excited to meet my baby, given that I was the only daughter in the family.

I, however, was in another world, still groggy from the sedation. Her words were the first to register my brain—a sweet, melodious voice that cut through the fog of my semi-conscious state.

As the sedation wore off and I began to regain my senses, I saw Parashar standing next to me. Although my eyes were heavy, I instantly recognized his touch. Gently, I asked him, 'Are you happy? You have a baby boy! Have you seen him? How does he look? Is he healthy?' My mind was swirling with questions, and I blurted all of them out.

Parashar was overjoyed and could barely speak. He just touched me softly and told me, 'All is well, and our baby is doing great.'

I pressed on. 'You wanted a healthy child. Is he healthy?'

He reassured me, 'Don't worry. You rest now. Our baby is healthy and being looked after by the nurses.'

'I have not seen him yet. Can you ask them to bring him to me?' I insisted.

He seemed surprised, assuming that I had already seen our baby. Without hesitation, he requested the nurses to bring our little boy.

And there he was—our little prince charming, our angel— wrapped in layers like a precious gift. He was fair, radiating a glow I had rarely seen in a child. I was too weak to hold him so the nurses laid him beside me. I drew him close and hugged him, holding Parashar's hands. It was a carpe diem moment for us—one we would treasure and relive countless times.

I experienced two different emotions in that moment. For me, it was an epiphany; alongside the delivery of my baby, I had also given birth to a new version of myself—the mother in me. It was a carpe diem moment for Parashar as well, as he would be able to cherish this experience and relive it countless times in his mind. He wanted a healthy baby and for me to be well, and he had been blessed with both.

An inner voice resonated within, reminding me of my satsang teachings. And so, I visualized him as a smiling, happy and healthy child. This first vision became his reality as the years unfolded.

◆

Vedant was born as a small-for-date baby, weighing just two kilograms. Any lower, he would have needed an incubator. But the collective prayers of all the spiritually aligned souls I was in touch with kept him protected.

It was 9 January 1998—a cold winter Friday in Kolkata. The doctor advised us to keep Vedant in the hospital for 10 days until the cold weather settled outside, allowing him to gain strength before venturing into the world outside.

It was then that I started discovering a new version of myself.

Although in excruciating pain due to the stitches, I refused to be dependent on others. I wanted to go to the toilet. When the nurses offered me a bedpan, I insisted on walking to the restroom. They were shocked and said the doctor had advised me to stay in bed on the first day. I assured them that nothing would happen to me.

With one nurse supporting me and another holding my saline drip, I slowly made my way to the toilet. The nurses were astonished. 'Ma'am,' they said, 'we have never seen a patient with a caesarean delivery get up on the same day. We were extremely reluctant to let you walk but you made us feel so proud. Your example will inspire others to push their limits.'

Their words filled me with pride. Even without a normal delivery, I had proven my strength to myself. In that moment, I realized I had conquered the first challenge of motherhood in my own unique way. It was a proud milestone—a new beginning that marked my rebirth as a mother. I was now waiting for my little boy—to hold him in my arms and bring him close to my bosom to experience the next intimate moment—nursing him.

From the first moment, he stole my heart—my little Prince Charming

Chapter 2

Exciting Beginnings

What truly defines motherhood is the feel of your newborn resting next to your bosom—an experience that remains etched forever!

I was waiting to hold my son in my arms. As a first-time mother, the experience was entirely new and overwhelming—a virgin experience that I knew I would cherish for a lifetime. The nurses had to teach me how to hold the baby in the proper nursing position. They explained the importance of the first feed, the precious colostrum—nature's way of building a newborn's immune system. Although Vedant was underweight and struggled to suckle effectively, the nurses showed me how to encourage him and emphasized how crucial it was for him to try, as the act of sucking stimulates milk production.

I think this was the most challenging part of my entire journey so far—nine months of carrying him had felt natural, but this was a whole new terrain. I perhaps shouldn't call it 'challenging'; maybe 'transformative' is the better word.

Nursing Vedant wasn't easy as he was a small baby. He would begin to suckle, only to fall asleep moments later. Waking him up was almost like a task. I remember the nurses sharing their 'tricks' with me, and I couldn't help but laugh. 'Manisha, tickle his soles to keep him awake; if that does not help, tickle him behind his earlobes. This will definitely help him stay awake!'

Even as I followed their advice, I found tears streaming down my cheeks—not of frustration, but of wonder. My heart whispered: 'This tiny, fragile creature of God has just emerged out of me; how could one ask him to do so much? He is so happily dependent on me; how can he be expected to put in so much effort so soon?'

In that moment, a voice within—a voice I believe was God's—spoke to me: 'Manisha, this little one is no longer in you; he has come through you, but he is not for you. He is an independent soul, and it is your responsibility to teach him to be independent. Teaching him to nurse is his first step towards independence, and there will be many more steps to follow.'

Sleepless nights followed as I nursed my little one. I never shed tears of anxiety but always of immense joy and pride. I felt blessed to be entrusted with this angel of God and to be a part of his journey towards independence.

◆

For all the expectant mothers or those planning to embark on this journey, here's one of my most profound learnings: Your life will never be yours anymore. There will always be an attachment—an eternal bond that is difficult to explain as you take birth again, this time as a 'mother'. It can only be experienced when the time is right, and I can vouch it will be worth every sleepless night and every moment.

As I nursed Vedant, I found myself becoming increasingly attached to him. He was fed, and I felt complete. His satisfaction brought me peace, and when he rested for a couple of hours, I too could relax. But soon, his cries would resume, demanding another feed, and the cycle continued endlessly.

Feeding him became my life's rhythm. I often joked to myself that I felt like a cow, constantly feeding and eating to sustain my energy for the next feed. Each session would last over an hour, and just when I thought I could rest, he'd be hungry again!

'What we serve, we get attached to, and it was, no doubt, one of the most exciting beginnings for me. I considered lactation to be the most sacred period after becoming a mother. Nursing him gave me a sense of fulfilment unlike anything else.'

During our Montessori course, we had studied that artificial nipples should not be given to young babies as they are not good for them. Initially, I was unable to express milk and store it in bottles. However, since Vedant was born underweight, the paediatrician advised me to gradually start expressing.

She told me, 'Manisha, if you do not express and store milk, you won't know how much the baby has consumed, and you will spend the entire day waiting for him to get the next feed without getting any rest for yourself. For the baby's development, please start expressing milk to monitor his intake. This will also give you some time to relax and come back to him rejuvenated.'

It made logical sense, though it was not something I embraced happily at first. Nonetheless, I accepted her advice with grace.

I realized that as a mother, it is important to prioritize what is appropriate for the child. Above all, breast milk was the only way for him to gain the necessary weight to move out of the 'small-for-date' category.

For the next five months, I followed this regimen religiously. During this time, he was entirely dependent on breast milk. I started expressing milk, storing it in bottles and feeding him with a baby spoon to ensure he had consumed an adequate quantity.

In 1998, expressing milk was done manually, as machines were not commonly used. Even when they were available, they could bruise the breasts, making it difficult for the baby to suckle. The process was laborious, but I persevered, knowing it was crucial for Vedant's health and growth.

I am sure my readers must be wondering why I am sharing such intricate details. I believe you won't find such details in any other book on motherhood. This is my personal journey, and I hope it helps many out there not to feel disheartened but to enjoy this exciting beginning of becoming a mother!

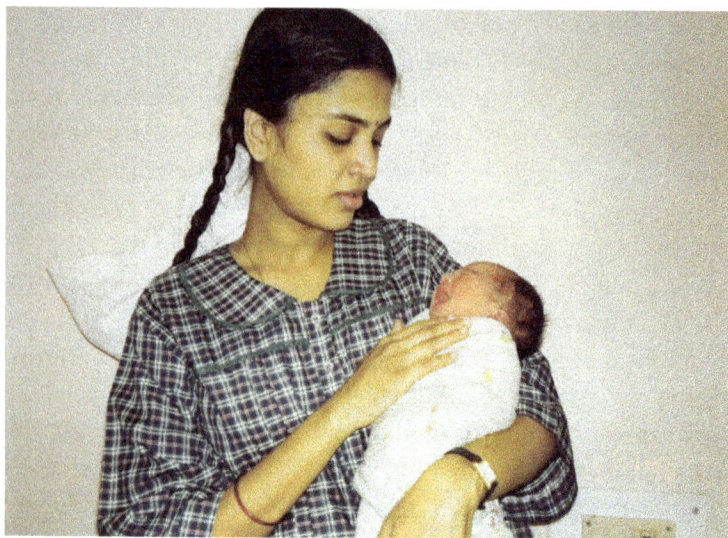

My world in my arms, my boy for life

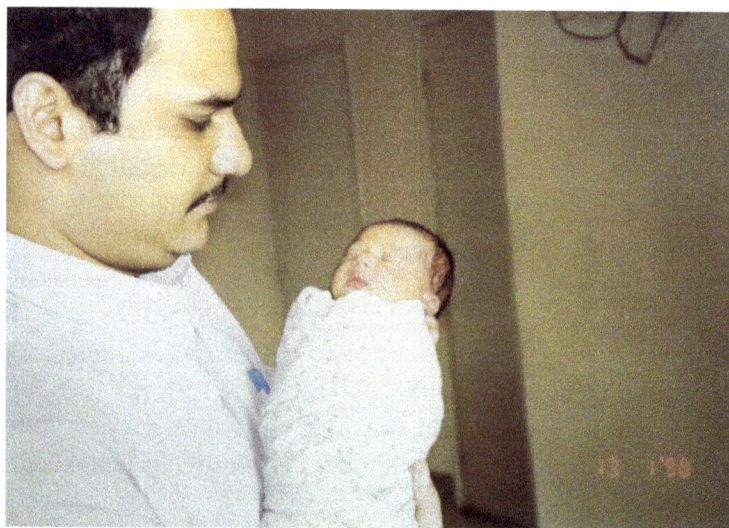

Two loves of my life, wrapped in one frame

Hey World, I am Coming!

Hey world, I am coming!
Catch me if you can.

I am learning to open
My two little eyes,
I am learning to move
My two little hands
I am just learning to learn.

Hey world, I am coming!
Catch me if you can.

I am independent now,
I hear a whisper—I guess it is my mom's voice,
A sound so familiar,
'Open your mouth, little one...'

Hey world, I am coming!
Catch me if you can.

I will learn to nourish myself,
I will learn to move my body.
I will learn to move my lips,
I will learn to take baby steps—
To walk, to run, to hop, to skip!

Hey world, I am coming!
Catch me if you can.

Skip a heartbeat with my tricks,
Surprise all with my gimmicks.
Running into a mess, yet being
Strong enough to face the world—
And to keep squealing with joy!

Hey world, I am coming!
None will be able to catch me.

Chapter 3

The Journey

Ibegin with a quote by Revered Mahātria as I feel there is a strong correlation with what I am about to pen down. 'The journey to the picnic should be as enjoyable as the picnic itself.'

Vedant was growing, and I was enjoying every moment of my journey with him. It was filled with joy and peace, as I held him, nurtured him and deepened my attachment to him.

The first five months as a mother were an emotional roller coaster. As Vedant completed five months, he reached his target weight, and we slowly introduced liquids and semi-solid foods into his diet.

Although I had helpers, I loved doing everything for him—from massaging and bathing him to preparing his juices and food. Every part of this journey was intriguing for me. My mother-in-law was of great help as she too believed that one of us should always be present to take care of him.

Something way beyond my expectations happened, which added a feather to my cap as a Montessorian. After my delivery, the Montessori institute approached me to become an examiner for the students undergoing training with them. To my surprise, I was sent essays written by the students for correction, for which I was paid! I was overjoyed and thrilled to receive such a blessing from God while still being at home. As I went through the essays, I felt deeply connected with the Montessori philosophy, and my love for children grew even more. Above all, my love grew each day for the little one I held in my arms.

The words of my beloved Guru resonated within me: 'Surpass your own expectations and surprise yourself at every step in this journey called Life.'

Questions flooded my mind: 'What are You preparing me for, my Lord!' immediately followed by, 'Why do You love me so much, my God!'

By the time Vedant was approaching his first birthday, I was still nursing him. My doctor advised me to slowly wean him off as my feed was no longer important for him. Nursing had become more about his seeking comfort and my emotional gratification. Lactation had created a deep bond between us, and the thought of weaning filled me with melancholy. Yet I knew it was my responsibility to help this little one become independent. This would be the second minuscule step towards his independence, and I needed to wean him off with peace.

In February 1999, we attended a family wedding in Varanasi when Vedant was a year and one month old. I was no longer nursing him by then so that he would be able to stay without me. Parashar and I had not taken a holiday for a long time, so we decided to extend our trip and go to Khajuraho after attending the wedding. By this time, I had successfully weaned Vedant, and with that, my monthly cycles returned.

To my utter surprise, in March 1999, I discovered that I had conceived again. I was taken aback and consulted our gynaecologist. He advised against continuing with the pregnancy, citing my frail health and the risks of sustaining another nine-month term so soon.

With great reluctance, we arranged for a D&C procedure* on 11 March 1999. Even my father, who strongly believed that children are sent by God and that we have no authority to terminate a pregnancy, agreed to the procedure, considering my health.

---

*Dilation and curettage (D&C) is a surgical procedure that removes tissue from the inside of the uterus.

Yet, my heart was heavy. I felt torn and conflicted. Having grown up surrounded by nephews and nieces, I had always envisioned a home bustling with children. Now, I was making a decision that went against everything I had ever dreamt of.

Back then, I was not acquainted with the silence of meditation or the guidance it could have offered. I relied on my inner connection with God to navigate this painful moment. I told myself that with Vedant being only a year old, it would be impossible to manage another baby. But now, as I reflect, I often wonder: 'Who am I to think that I am taking care of the child? When God decides to give a child, He ensures everything needed to care for that child.'

Nevertheless, what had to be done was done. It left me in a state of complete shock and despair. To this day, I have not fully forgiven myself for that act. I try to console myself with thoughts like: 'Maybe the child would not have been fit to come into this world...' Yet I continue to feel the absence of a second child—a sibling for Vedant.

Soon after, in 2000, we moved to Chennai—a new city and a new chapter in my life. But the third initiation into motherhood never happened for me, even though I deeply yearned for it.

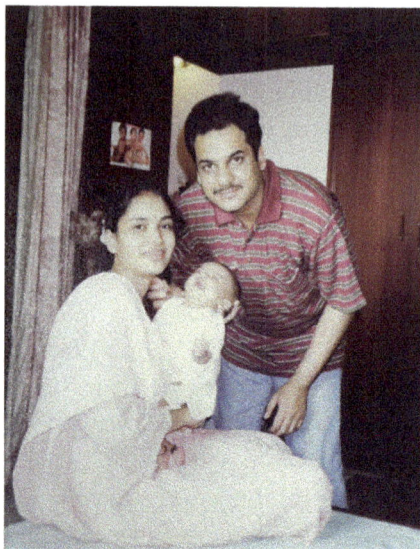

A happy family

Wrapped in Mumma's arms

Chapter 4

Play with Your Body

After my D&C in March 1999, I was prescribed multiple medicines to cope with the ensuing bout of depression. In August of the same year, we visited London for the first time with Vedant, who was then one and a half years old. During this trip, my brother learnt about the procedure and became extremely angry at me and Dad.

His words still reverberate within me as I write this, and tears trickle down my cheeks… I pause. I have never been able to fully forgive myself. No words of wisdom or moments of silence have healed that pain. Yet, somewhere deep within, I knew my journey would touch lives one day.

Having grown up in a household where Swami Vivekananda and Sri Ramakrishna Paramhansa were revered, I found it easier to maintain my balance and integrity, even when I felt life was not going in the right direction. I consoled myself with the thought that this was a part of His plan, and His plan is always right!

Images of Sri Ramakrishna Paramhansa at the lotus feet of Maa Kali adorned our home, and my father, an ardent follower of Swami Vivekananda, instilled in us the strength to embrace life's trials with grace. Birthday celebrations in our home were marked not by parties or fancy gifts but by books—endless books on values, growth and spirituality, spanning all religions. We lived by the ethos of 'play with your body', with a reflection of Swami Vivekananda's words: 'Muscles of iron and nerves of steel, inside which dwells a mind of the same material as that of which the thunderbolt is made.'

These principles became a part and parcel of my physical, intellectual, emotional and spiritual well-being. Although I was unsettled by the sudden relocation and the lingering grief of the abortion, staying connected to these values reinvigorated me to face life's challenges. I realized I needed to consciously nurture my inner being to give my best to Vedant.

Now I can understand the relevance of Revered Mahātria's saying: 'You are never given an experience that is not needed for your own evolution.' The shift to Chennai was indeed essential for my growth.

Interestingly, God's plan unfolded in unexpected ways. My Montessori teacher from Kolkata, Mrs Raghavan, had retired and relocated to Chennai a year prior. She became my only point of contact in this new environment.

I reached out to her at a time when mobile phones were not yet ubiquitous. She advised that I should enrol Vedant in a good preschool nearby to help him develop social skills through interaction with his peers. She assured me I could introduce him to basic Montessori methods at home rather than lamenting the lack of a Montessori house nearby.

Taking her advice, I enrolled Vedant in a playschool and used the free time to set up a Montessori-inspired environment at home. The philosophy of Dr Maria Montessori had transformed me as an individual, and I saw this as an opportunity to direct my energy towards Vedant's development.

I converted a room in our house into a mini-Montessori set-up using basic household items. Each activity in the Montessori methodology was presented to Vedant in a way that enhanced his sensory development and prepared him for life. Activities like rolling and unrolling mats, picking up and placing chairs, or even holding a pencil correctly might seem trivial, but they align a child's mind and body systematically, nurturing lifelong skills.

Our mornings were dedicated to Vedant's time at preschool,

where he honed his social skills. The afternoons post lunch and siesta, from 3 p.m. to 5 p.m., turned into our Montessori sessions.

Revered Mahātria's words became my guiding mantra: 'Any deprivation in the world—you should be the one to complete it, not complain about it. Take responsibility, work on the cause, and the effect will follow.'

With that spirit in mind, I embraced this new responsibility to guide Vedant in Montessori lessons. By creating the environment, imparting the training and embodying the values of an early childhood educator, I fulfilled my dual role as his mother and mentor.

Evenings, however, were reserved for joy and activities. We would visit the nearby park to freely move our bodies, often engaging in games, running and practising yoga together. This phase of my life became a testament to the transformative power of inner discipline, love and unwavering faith in God's greater plan.

Cheering from the sidelines, right beside my little champion

That First Heartbeat

That first heartbeat,
Paused everything for me—
For a moment, I froze;
Everything seemed still.

It took me into a realm,
Where nothing seemed to exist
But me and the rhythm.

Lub-dub, lub-dub went the beat,
Resonating within,
Changing everything for me,
Silencing all inner noise!

All of that first heartbeat,
Formed within weeks;

Yet enduring forever,
As long as life itself.
It is the heartbeat—
The pulse of existence.

In one moment it begins;
In one moment it can stop.
Unbelievably divine,
Born unknowingly within.

It can only be heard
When the world grows quiet,
When moments pause—
Calling humanity to rise,
To shine above the ordinary!

Dissolve your ego,
Unwind the unknown path.
Let the heart's rhythm guide you:
Lub-dub, lub-dub.
It is that first heartbeat,
Created in a mother's womb,
An echo of the unmanifested within,
To make all of us create like the Creator does.

I was moved to hear it beat,
What have I done to deserve this!
Yet, I longed to keep hearing it beat.

Not realizing that it could only be
Heard in stillness,
In quieting our restless mind.
That is when we hear the sound within:
'Be still and know your God.'

Children are next to God,
To feel God, to feel the child
Within, we have to be still;
We are all children,
Children of the Supreme!
God created me as you
And you as me.
In each one of us, there is God—
He can hear our heart beat
As I heard that first heartbeat!

I feel so responsible,
So accountable, holding a
Life within. I must live it to the hilt.
And for me, living to the hilt
Is to think good, to speak good,
And doing good for all.
For we are made by God,
And He makes our hearts beat,
As I heard that first heartbeat within.

He hears it in Him, as long as we live;
I heard it in me, a life forming within,
Reminding we have a purpose to fulfil.

It is His will to bless us with life;
It is His will to take it away.
But it is on us, how we choose
To live this human life—
To keep hearing
That first heartbeat!

Chapter 5

Horizontal Exposure, Vertical Expertise

To push ourselves beyond our comfort zone, there has to be horizontal exposure—exploring a variety of experiences—to gradually develop vertical expertise in an area our heart truly connects with!

Children, especially at a young age, benefit from such varied exposure. It helps them discover their true passion. In a Montessori house, children between the ages of two and six work together, creating a unique environment of mutual growth. It has a very strong impact on the subconscious mind of a child. Younger children learn by observing their older peers. When their time comes, they are able to master these skills easily. Meanwhile, the older children develop compassion and empathy as they guide the younger ones.

Montessori learning had become a part of my being. Implementing its principles came effortlessly. When Vedant turned three and a half years old, he completed one year at Spring Blossoms playschool. Immediately after, we were able to enrol him in Sharanalaya Montessori School, recently opened by Smita Vishweshwar, which was fairly close to our house.

I was very happy about Vedant finally going to a Montessori house. While mornings were spent there, evenings were reserved for his physical activities and sports classes. Vedant's hands-on learning continued; after all the activities of the day got over, he spent time in the Montessori room I had set up in the house.

Vedant began learning lawn tennis at a nearby tennis court, which was located close to our house. I did not want him travelling long distances in the evening as the traffic would be heavy. Tennis became a natural extension of his bond with balls—a connection I first noticed when he was two and a half months old. At that time, seeing a ball on the bed, he instinctively turned to reach for it—another carpe diem moment I hold on to!

I owe my father immense gratitude for instilling the importance of physical activity in us from a young age. It enabled me to pass the same values to Vedant at the right time. It is very important for mothers to go through the right learning at the right stage as they play a pivotal role in shaping a child's future. A mother's learning and conditioning significantly influences the child, especially during the formative years. Revered Mahātria's words resonate deeply here: 'Human beings are a product of their past conditioning.'

From the prenatal stage to age six, a child absorbs 75 per cent of what they need to learn! The environment we expose them to shapes their foundation for life.

While Vedant's Montessori training was underway, my father-in-law found a place near our residence for me to start a Montessori house for children. I was hesitant as I wanted to gain some teaching experience elsewhere before venturing out on my own. Vedant was still young and needed much of my time and attention. Establishing and managing a Montessori house required immense focus and dedication, for which I felt unprepared at that stage.

However, my father-in-law was adamant. He saw my passion for early childhood education and assured me that he, along with Parashar, would manage the finances. I had to focus solely on creating and managing the Montessori environment.

Though I was reluctant, I got in touch with Mrs Raghavan, who agreed to come on board as the advisor and manage the nuances of setting up the environment. To my relief, she lived close to the place we found, and her guidance in procuring materials, recruiting staff and setting up the environment was invaluable. She was very happy to join me in my new venture. I closed my eyes in awe—God's ways are His ways; we can only accept with grace whatever He blesses us with!

With her support and God's favour, Vatsalya Montessori House was born on the auspicious day of Vijayadashami in October 2002. It marked the beginning of a journey to provide 'horizontal exposure and vertical expertise' to children.

Vedant continued his Montessori education at Sharanalaya, engaging in sports and developing a habit of reading books. I deliberately refrained from enrolling him at Vatsalya. Familiarity with the environment, especially seeing his mother there, might have hindered his development as a Montessori child. He needed to step out of his comfort zone and be in an external environment to grow exponentially. It was a tough decision, but that is what motherhood entails—making choices that prioritize the child's long-term growth.

For all mothers—young, soon-to-be or even those who wish to conceive—I strongly recommend studying the Montessori method. It develops a profound understanding of children and instils respect for them as independent beings. Let us realize that education begins at birth!

School life begins—Vedant in Class 1

Chapter 6

Firm Grip, Soft Gloves

'A place for everything and everything in its place.'

This principle imparted to children during their sensitive years (two to six) stays with them for life. It also played a pivotal role in shaping Vedant as a young adult. The grace and excellence with which he maintained orderliness often surprised me and exceeded my expectations. His Montessori journey—starting with lessons absorbed in my womb, continuing at home and Sharanalaya—instilled a natural inclination to organize his surroundings. Even as a child, he tidied his room by himself and returned things to their original places.

My personal growth through the Montessori philosophy had changed my inner being and my parenting approach. It was hard for me to scold Vedant. Yet, as a mother, I had to be stern with him at times while nurturing him with softness.

The phrase 'firm grip, soft gloves' is very close to my heart. It embodies the ideal parenting style—firm enough to provide direction, yet soft enough to ensure the child feels loved. My eldest brother, Hemant, had explained its relevance to me in interacting with everyone, whether children or adults. Watching him and Dad seamlessly combine authority with affection as entrepreneurs made this trait my second nature.

Vedant was growing fast, and I often found myself wanting to pause time, holding on to his childhood moments. A close friend once told me, 'Manisha, enjoy every moment now. Children grow up so fast and soon, all you will have are memories to cherish.'

As I write, I feel tears of joy and pride. I have treasured every moment with Vedant, creating a collection of carpe diem moments. All I have to do is close my eyes and they play before me like a video!

I encourage every parent to pause often and spend quality time with their children. Relish these moments now, for they will become the treasures you live with later.

◆

Vedant studied at Bhavan's Rajaji Vidyashram till class two, which was also close to our house. He continued playing tennis and his journey through coaching centres was far from linear. He always had some story that would compel me to change his coaching centre.

One day, he told me, 'Maa, someone called me *goondu*. I will not go there again.' Someone had called him fat.

I replied, 'Call him *patlu* next time.' His eyes sparkled as he found solace in the playful retaliation I suggested.

I realized children, especially at a young age, seek to be heard with empathy. When we acknowledge their feelings and offer simple solutions for their so-called problems, they feel on top of the world!

Children deserve to feel special, as it is important to preserve the innocence they carry. I applied this understanding with Vedant by never insisting that he stay in an environment where he felt uncomfortable. While I took the time to explain things to him, if he still felt unsettled, I changed the location and continued with the centre of his preference. I realized if I pushed him at that age, he would develop a negative attitude towards the sport. Fortunately, when I switched his coaching centre, he began to love tennis and connected with an excellent teacher. Through this experience, I learnt that by respecting his feelings—even when they didn't seem very logical to me as an adult—I was able to gain his trust and nurture his love for the sport.

◆

Vedant's disciplined life with a proper routine underwent a major shift when we enrolled him into Sishya, ranked among the top schools in India. Its reputation reminded me of La Martinière, the iconic school my husband and I attended in Kolkata.

Enrolling Vedant at Sishya wasn't an easy decision. The school was about 45 minutes away, so the commute posed a major challenge. My in-laws and Parashar were opposed to sending Vedant to a school that was so far. Yet I felt strongly about giving Vedant the opportunity to study there.

To convince Vedant to take the admission test, I had to be creative. I told him that if he passed the test, he would win tickets to the animated movie *Hanuman*. Given his love for religious cartoons based on Lord Krishna, the *Ramayana*, Lord Ganesha and Lord Hanuman, this served as the perfect motivation.

As part of their expansion, Sishya was adding one section per class, intending to admit 20 students for each section. Vedant enthusiastically agreed to sit for the preliminary maths and language tests in lieu of the tickets.

I pre-booked the tickets and took him to the movie once the test was over.

I needed to get him excited about the test in order for him to perform well. If I had mentioned that it was for a change of schools, he would have refused to participate and likely would have intentionally messed up the test! At that age, children become very comfortable with their friends and surroundings. Changing schools requires their readiness and adaptability to the new situation.

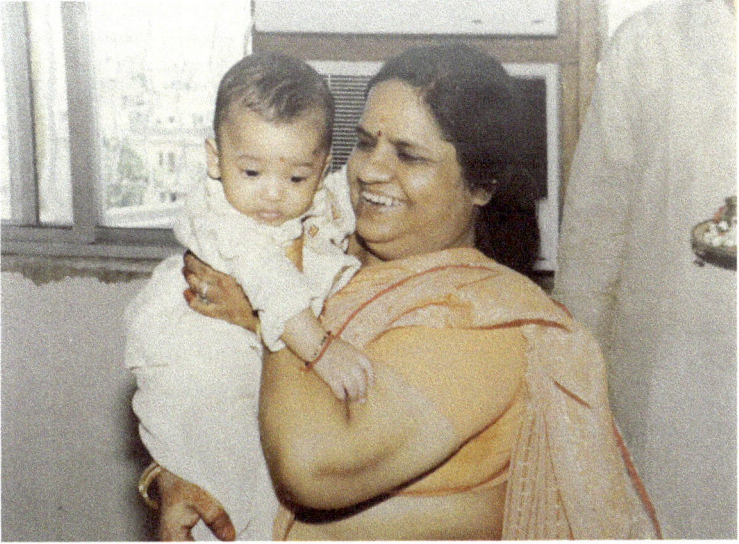

Vedant and his grandmother—her little shona

Unison

Love, love, love—
How magical art thou!
Thou touches a soul,
Transforming its very being.

Love, love, love—
How enterprising art thou!
Thou engulfs a human,
Changing its very chemistry.

Love, love, love—
How enduring can you be!
Instilling patience within;
A willingness always to give, to serve.

Love, love, love—
Have you ever thought of self?
Do words like 'self', 'me', 'myself' exist?
It comes not even for a fraction.

For me, that is love—
As I feel blessed to feel love,
As I have been touched by love.
Love is not a mere word but real.

It is in feeling God's love;
With a God who walks beside,
With a God who touches beings infinite,
With a God who lives with and within.

I feel blessed to feel God within,
In my inner chambers residing,
Communing with me in silence,
As vibrations, as echoes, as words.

Flowing through poetry, through music,
In dance, as an eternal rhythm within,
Going on and on for eternity,
Silencing all lips that pledge to speak!

People lined up in long queues,
Yearning for a darshan of their Lord,
As the curtain of the shrine parts,
A hush falls, Divinity captured within!

'Tis a scene to behold,
That a naked eye oft cannot,
It happens only with God's grace!
To engulf Him, as the veil unveils.

Life appears His divine leela,
As his image is captured within,
Human frailty dissolves, love gushes in…
Ego vanishes, surrender becomes all!

God's grace touches infinite souls,
Lifting them beyond me, mine, myself,
To serve a higher purpose, a noble cause
To unite many with their One!

That, to me, is unison—
To feel one with Him and dissolve,
In God, in love, and in all beings,
Possible only with His divine radiance!

Chapter 7

Tongue-Conscious or Health-Conscious

Vedant successfully passed the admission test for Sishya and settled comfortably in his new school from the very first day. I recall the wise words of Mrs Raghavan: 'Children adapt to their environment very easily—it is we, as adults, who take time.' Her statement resonated deeply with me, especially during our move to Chennai, when I was apprehensive about how Vedant would adjust to a new city.

Her words proved to be profoundly true as Vedant not only adapted quickly to Chennai but also embraced his new school environment with ease.

The only drawback was the school's distance—close to an hour from our home. This required meticulous preparation each morning to ensure he was ready and left on time. It indirectly taught both of us to manage our daily routine more effectively.

Vedant joined the third standard in Sishya, skipping the latter half of the second standard. Unlike Bhavan's, which followed an academic year starting in June, Sishya's session began in January. It gave him the advantage of transitioning early.

Dr Thomas, a well-known gastroenterologist and the founder of Sishya, personally interviewed the parents as part of the admission process. During the interview, he had asked me, 'Mrs Lohia, do you ensure your child has breakfast before leaving for school?'

I replied, 'Sir, he has an apple, some almonds and a glass of milk.'

Dr Thomas emphasized, 'Breakfast is the most important meal of the day. It fuels their focus and helps them concentrate in school. Often, children miss eating their tiffin during snack breaks, leaving them sluggish by the end of the day. Please ensure Vedant eats breakfast each morning before coming to school.'

His words resonated with me, and my respect for his wisdom grew. We had never had a proper breakfast in our growing years; it usually comprised milk, a fruit and some almonds—a tradition I had continued with Vedant. Dr Thomas's advice marked a turning point, and I adopted the habit of preparing a wholesome breakfast for Vedant daily.

His next concern was about something both Vedant and I struggled with till he completed his schooling. 'Mrs Lohia, we do not allow latecomers into the school. How will you ensure Vedant arrives on time every day, given the distance from Anna Nagar is nearly 50 minutes?'

I replied with conviction, 'Sir, I will make sure he is in school on time every day.'

We soon got to know that Vedant had done well in his test, and my husband and I had also passed the interview with Dr Thomas. This marked the beginning of our journey with Sishya!

I cherished every moment—preparing him for school, curating his tiffin and engaging him in extracurricular activities. Each task made me feel super excited; I gave my best to every moment, living to the hilt.

However, with all the love Vedant received from his grandparents, he started gaining weight. Coming from a family where healthy eating and physical fitness were strongly encouraged, I had always been mindful of what I consumed while ensuring I regularly exercised. My father instilled in us the value of choosing food that would nourish the body and fuel the mind.

On the other hand, the Marwari food habits on my in-laws' side leaned towards indulging in fried and spicy dishes. Following my father-in-law's bypass surgery immediately after my marriage, dietary changes were necessary but not easy to adapt to, as they were accustomed to their traditional cuisine. Food also became a way for them to dote on Vedant. Ice creams, pizzas, burgers and cakes were offered in abundance as tokens of love, though I often felt they indulged more for their own joy than his.

I remained steadfast in my approach. Following the Montessori philosophy, I believed that to guide Vedant, I first had to exemplify the habits I wanted him to adopt. 'Practice what you preach' became my mantra! Children learn much more from what they see than from what they hear.

My routine revolved around ensuring Vedant received balanced meals and engaged in physical activity. Each morning began with a carefully planned breakfast, followed by school, where his tiffin was thoughtfully curated to balance taste and nutrition. Post-school hours included studies, assignments, and either a joint physical activity or sports. Despite these efforts, Vedant's weight continued to increase, even as he progressed from primary to secondary school.

Parents, grandparents and our little star—Vedant completes us

Chapter 8

Practice What You Preach!

*'Do not tell them how to do it. Show them how to do it
and do not say a word. If you tell them,
they will watch your lips move. If you show them,
they will want to do it themselves.'*

—Dr Maria Montessori

Living as a Montessorian meant striving for grace and excellence
in all that I did—from the moment I woke to the time I retired
for the day. As Revered Mahātria says, 'Grace is something we
bring to every act of ours, and excellence is what we carry within
us, which defines our personality.'

I vividly remember my days as a Montessori student, where
small yet meaningful practices like aligning our footwear neatly
at the threshold or sitting on mats for activities were emphasized
upon. These seemingly simple acts were imbued with deeper
lessons of order, respect and mindfulness.

I wonder at times how Dr Maria Montessori conceptualized
something as intricate as this philosophy! It is a science—a
holistic approach to living life positively from the earliest stage,
even when the baby is in the womb.

Reflecting on how life led me to learn and embrace this
philosophy fills me with gratitude and responsibility. I feel
compelled to share these teachings with parents, children and
everyone in my environment.

When we embody these values, the impact radiates beyond ourselves. Revered Mahātria beautifully captures this idea: 'When we stay in a rose garden long enough, we smell roses wherever we go.' Similarly, when we live with grace and purpose, the people around us are inspired to adopt those qualities, even unconsciously.

Starting young is pivotal, and this is where Montessori plays a transformative role. For Vedant, having a Montessorian mother meant being immersed in an environment where positive habits and values were naturally integrated into daily life. While he might not have had a choice, his upbringing ensured he adopted these principles effortlessly.

I prioritized spending quality time with Vedant over social outings, focusing on activities that would nurture his growth. Whether it was engaging in physical activities, reading or simply exploring new things together, every moment was a chance to bond and grow. Vedant, in turn, pushed me to step out of my comfort zone. For example, when we went swimming, he would challenge me to a race and I would try to be the first to reach the other side!

◆

Vedant was growing up to be a very accepting child. He was nearing eight years and our shared goal was addressing his weight gain. Daily physical activities of his choice and a nutritious diet became central to our routine. Between ages two and eight, Vedant explored various sports like football, basketball and lawn tennis.

While his life in Sishya was going on in full swing, I made sure that he participated in important family occasions too. With both sides of our families spread across Kolkata, Delhi and London, I wanted him to bond with his cousins and uncles. Vedant being my only child, I felt it was important for him to spend quality time with the extended family. Sishya respected the importance of such horizontal exposure for the child, approving leaves for significant family events.

When Vedant reached grade five, my niece's wedding in Kolkata coincided with his half-yearly exams. For the first time, he had to study on his own as I would be out of town for a few days. While his performance dipped slightly, it was a turning point—he gained confidence and began studying on a regular basis, approaching his dad, grandmother or me for assistance when he needed help.

My mother-in-law is very proficient in Hindi. I made sure that Vedant studied with his grandmother so that a close bond would develop between them. Apart from teaching him, she also imparted many important values to him. Thanks to her dedication and effort, Vedant consistently topped his Hindi exams.

I believe that a child's love for a subject depends on how it is taught, and his grandmother was certainly one of his best teachers. It is truly a blessing when children grow up with their grandparents; the learnings they receive is truly irreplaceable.

Vedant was subconsciously absorbing everything necessary for his growth. The only concern was the extra weight he was carrying. However, as a mother, I was confident that he would be able to shed it with time. A mother's intuition is very strong, especially since her baby grows inside her for nine months.

Just the two of us—Vedant and Mumma, always

A Realization

From the depths of slumber,
I heard a voice whispering.
It seemed to me familiar,
Speaking in faint murmurs.
This voice lingered with and within.
Echoing through the deepest chambers,
Revealing something fascinating, something unknown.

From the depths of slumber,
I heard footsteps approaching.
It seemed to me a known sound,
Guiding and showing me around,
As this sound lingered with and within
The inner chambers to reveal to me,
Something I had long concealed, worth uncovering.

From the depths of slumber,
I heard birds chirping.
It seemed to me from a known land,
Calling me from a higher branch to drop
The lower one and climb towards heights unknown.
I knew not where I would be going, but climbing,
On and on, ascending, as I realized it to be the Divine!

From the depths of slumber,
I realized it was God's voice,

Talking to me, vibrating in my ears,
Telling me, 'I am in you, my child;
I have come to you as a realization!
To awaken you to your true essence,
To shed the mortal shell and become Divine!'

Chapter 9

Show Your Child Narayana at an Early Age

What we leave our children is not material wealth but rich moral and ethical values that become their guiding light through life. Introducing your child to Narayana at an early age instils in them a spiritual anchor—a force that leads them through every moment of storm and calm in life.

Maa had shown me Narayana early in my life, and as a mother, I sought to do the same for Vedant. The mother's role is crucial in shaping a child's life, especially during their formative years, as she spends most of the time with them, leaving an indelible influence that lasts for a lifetime.

Vedant's birth was a blessing from Professor Prema Pandurang. Her unwavering faith in Narayana fortified mine, especially during those transitional phases of marriage that challenge every woman. She constantly reminded me to place my trust in Lord Krishna, strengthening my resolve and helping me navigate life's uncertainties.

With this surrender, Vedant entered my life, and I have always regarded him as a child of God. During my pregnancy, I loved listening to bhajans, reading scriptures and attending spiritual discourses. God has always been my closest companion. This innate connection with the Divine flowed effortlessly to Vedant as he observed and absorbed the same practices.

Vedant grew up calling Professor Prema Pandurang 'Prema

nanimaa'—a privilege very few children had. He often dressed as baby Krishna during her Bhagavad discourses, captivating audiences who saw him as an incarnation of Lord Krishna. Vedant bore an uncanny resemblance to a photograph of baby Krishna that my father had given me when he got to know about my pregnancy.

In our Indian culture, it is believed that if a childless couple touches the feet of baby Krishna, they will be blessed with a son like him. On the day of Lord Krishna's birth, amidst the seven-day discourse conducted by Professor Prema Pandurang, people thronged to touch Vedant's feet, as he was dressed as baby Krishna!

If this was not a blessing then what could be? Such moments left me speechless and moved me to tears of gratitude. I often whispered silent prayers to God: 'Thank you, my God, for blessing me with this human experience. Thank you, my God, for blessing me with a child through whom I can connect with You. Thanks to Your grace and blessings!'

Vedant grew up spending weekends watching the *Ramayana*, the *Mahabharata* and Krishna cartoons with his grandparents. Even when travelling across time zones, he would wake up early on Sunday mornings to watch his beloved Krishna serials, much to the annoyance of his cousins, who would rather sleep in. Unfazed, Vedant gently urged them to let him watch, saying, 'I'll miss my Krishna serial. Please, can you sleep in another room?' In complete abandon, he would continue watching the serial while everyone else slept soundly on a relaxed Sunday morning in a foreign country. He knew all the names and stories from every serial. It was as if he were a religious pundit, a fact that filled me with awe as a mother. These were moments worth living for!

At times, I would yearn for another child as I felt having a sibling was very important for a healthy upbringing. However, my homoeopathic doctor, whom I revere as a father figure, once told me, 'Manisha, be grateful that you have a child; there are many who are childless. Stop thinking of what you do not have. Focus your energy on raising Vedant well so that others may learn from your parenting. Through him, you can touch countless lives.'

His words were an epiphany for me, which essentially shifted my perspective. I stopped asking God for anything from then on. I realized, 'When we ask God for something, He gives us only that. But when we do not ask for anything, what He gives is according to His choice and will.'

This awakening deepened my resolve to raise Vedant with even stronger values. When he was barely nine, he dressed as Swami Vivekananda to deliver a speech at the World Confluence on Humanity, Power and Spirituality that my father had organized. The event saw leaders from diverse religions assemble from across the globe, with the sole objective of promoting a feeling of oneness among all and propagating the shared essence of all religious teachings.

Vedant not only met but exceeded all expectations, embodying the message of oneness and harmony with conviction and grace. Moments like these reaffirmed my belief in divine providence and the incredible potential within a child who is nurtured with love, faith and values.

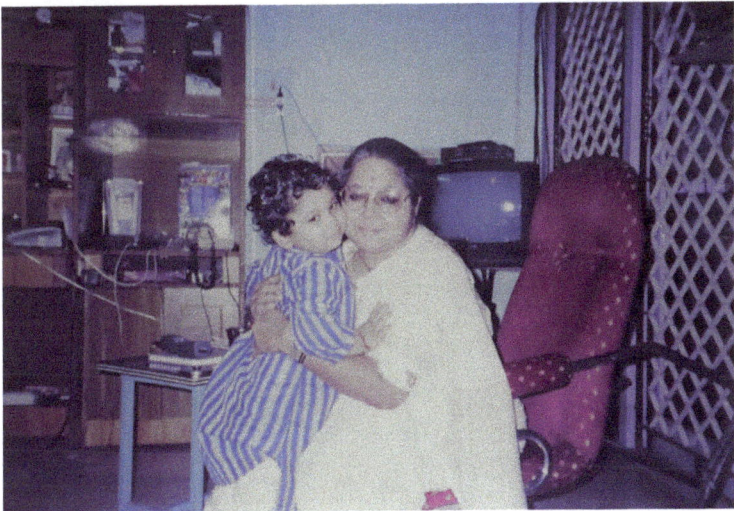

Blessed by his favourite—Prema Nanimaa's love surrounds Vedant

Our little Krishna

Devotion begins young

Chapter 10

Letting Go, Letting God In

'There are no suppositions in faith and
no negotiations in surrender.'

Chubby little Vedant often felt self-conscious about going on stage because of his weight. As his mother, I had to push him and motivate him, assuring him he would excel on stage with his performance. He would tell me, 'Maa, if I eat like you, I will lose this extra weight. Then I will not feel so shy on stage.'

Holding back tears, I would hug him tightly and reassure, 'Vedant, you will achieve that too, but for now, just be confident. Close your eyes, think of Swami Vivekananda, surrender to God and perform. You will get a standing ovation!'

Vedant had complete faith in me and God, which ensured he performed with conviction. Each time, his remarkable delivery and presence left the audience stunned, earning him the admiration he deserved.

To prepare him for the speech, I chose a verse from one of Swami Vivekananda's books, memorized it and then taught it to Vedant by making him repeat after me. Through this, I realized that in faith, there are no suppositions, and in surrender, there are no negotiations.

It was my father's wish to have Vedant dress up as Swami Vivekananda and recite his wise words. Given Dad's experience, I knew he was doing the right thing for Vedant and that this would be a valuable opportunity for his grandson. Shaping young minds with the right values is crucial, as every positive input manifests in their lives in profound ways.

Dressing up as Swami Vivekananda and internalizing his teachings began to instil those values in Vedant. They say we become what we think of, and Vedant's emulation of the great Swami extended to his thoughts, actions, persona and, eventually, to his essence.

◆

Vedant was in class four at the time and was excelling in his studies. We had a dedicated study hour in the evenings after his school and sports activities. Later, either Parashar or I would read to him before he dozed off. Despite his young age, there was a lot to learn from Vedant in the way he kept his room tidy and clean. 'Everything in its place and a place for everything' was his mantra. If I teased him by misplacing something in his room, he would sternly say, 'Maa, please do not mess with the things in my room.'

His tidiness, a reflection of his Montessori upbringing, left me both amused and in awe. It felt as though Vedant had absorbed these traits even before birth, as I pursued my studies during pregnancy. His deep connection to the values of Prahlada, the young devotee of Lord Vishnu, felt symbolic. Just as Prahlada developed his devotion while in his mother's womb—nurtured by her own faith—I felt that Vedant, too, had imbibed this quality while growing within me.

I loved spending time with Vedant after his school hours and ensured I completed all my tasks before he returned. My main focus was to give him healthy food so that he refrained from eating junk. I prepared a weekly menu for him. After his evening sports activities, I would bring a snack—fruit, something light and a glass of milk—to keep him energized until dinner.

However, I often faced challenges with my in-laws, whose love for Vedant was expressed through indulgent sweets and fast food.

In India, food is synonymous with love, and chubby little Vedant was their perfect excuse for dessert outings. To counterbalance this, I ensured he ate healthy and nutritious food at home and was engaged in productive activities—playing games, reading and exploring intellectual curiosities appropriate for his age—to avoid unnecessary screen time and extravagant eating with his grandparents.

Despite my efforts, Vedant continued to put on weight, which sometimes worried me. Yet I clung to my faith in myself and God to overcome whatever obstacle came my way, accepting it with grace and complete surrender. I believe God sends guidance through His angels, and when we hold on to faith, He blesses us with the wisdom to recognize those angels.

One such angel appeared in the form of a classmate's mother. During a chance meeting, she mentioned her child was enrolled in a squash academy. Inspired, I signed Vedant up for squash, and this turned out to be the greatest blessing for both of us. Vedant fell in love with the sport and started looking forward to his after-school squash sessions every evening. I too got some time to read, walk in the park and just be with him. For me, Vedant has always been my priority. Beyond being his mother, I aimed to be his sibling, his best friend and his greatest cheerleader.

The cutest little apple on his big day—Vedant's first graduation

Vedant dressed as Swami Vivekananda

My Little One

Here goes the story of my little one—Vedant is his name.
He is 11 years old now,
No longer so little, yet, to me, he will always be.
And so, my story goes on.

A young, vibrant person am I,
Full of life and energy,
Wanting to study, become successful
Like my father and brothers are.
Aspirations filled my heart,
But God had His own plans for me.

He sent a charming young man,
Who stole my heart and asked for my hand.
There I was, stepping into the space all
Girls dream of! But my dream was a little different.

I dreamt of work, of learning, of
Doing something outstanding.
Always staying aligned with GOD,
My home, my new family gave me all that,
I plunged into studying again.

But not the conventional one,
One which would connect me to children,

In whom I would see God and would get the
Alignment of still being connected with God.

Why do I say God, God, God again and again?
I realize that was the oft heard word in the house—
Maa, my most adorable angel, always held faith in God.

I started my journey as an educator for young ones,
Two and a half decades back; life changed for me when
I conceived my little one in the last month of my course's
completion.

The sacred nine months—
How callously some let them pass,
But for me, they were a revelation.
They brought me closer to the One within,
Connecting me with God always,
What I thought was love, was faith in God!

How, why did He choose me to be worthy
To carry a life within?
Would I do justice to this sanctity?
Would I be ever ruthless to this life?
Or would I preserve this relationship,
For eternity and guide many to treasure theirs too!
I realized I was worthy, for the teachings ingrained
Within every cell of mine, to devote myself
To this life and nourish him as God.
This privilege is given to those who surrender to His will.

My little one, a bundle of joy is he,
Within my womb I could see him,
I could feel him as he kicked with all his might,
A boxer before birth, a footballer after!
It ignited sparks of happiness within!

Every month taught me,
First, to look after my health,
As that should be the primary focus.
My body, mind and soul had to be aligned,
My energy levels had to be at their peak,
My diet had to be light—not for two but enough
As much as my body could take.
I was active, alert and appreciative,
Towards all the goodness around,
The months passed into seconds.

I graduated as a Montessorian,
I graduated to become a mother,
Both came hand in hand.
The learnings complemented me as
I still grow with my little one of 11!

Chapter 11

Celebration Is Life

Vedant turned 11 on 9 January 2009. Double digits and that too 11—so it had to be special! Every birthday of his, since he turned three, has been a celebration. However, I had a very different approach to celebrating birthdays for small children.

During my Montessori course, Mrs Raghavan explained that a child in the age of one or two often feels overwhelmed by a large gathering. Celebrations at that age tend to be more for the parents' satisfaction than for the child's joy. She advised celebrating birthdays when the child is old enough to move around and understand the event.

This made absolute sense to me, and I adopted this perspective for Vedant. The first birthday we celebrated of his was when he turned four. As I pondered how to celebrate his birthday, a thought struck!

I wanted him to learn the names of different animals, so I planned a jungle-themed party. At four, children love animals and can easily identify their traits and sounds. I designed an invitation card by pasting pictures of animals, painting around them to give a lush, jungle-like look and added a note for the invite. This one idea sparked many others.

Inspired by the invitation, I created rectangular mats with similar designs, which could serve as a dining arrangement for the party and later be used daily.

From then on, every birthday—from four to 11 and beyond—

became a cherished celebration, not just for Vedant but also for his friends and their mothers. Each birthday had a unique theme that reflected either a learning I wanted him to pick up or something he was extremely fond of.

His fifth birthday was inspired by the animated movie *Hanuman*, which he adored. I crafted Hanuman-themed keychains with messages as invitation cards and matching table mats.

His sixth birthday party was Garfield-themed birthday and for or his seventh birthday, we had a *Titanic*-themed party. We had a dinosaur-themed birthday party to celebrate his eighth birthday and a musical instruments-themed party on his ninth to celebrate his budding interest in music. I introduced him to various instruments, among which he chose to play the tabla. We later found a tabla teacher for him. To mark his 'graduation' into double digits, I designed a scroll certificate as invitations for his 10th birthday. We made him wear graduation robes and clicked photographs, which were included in the invites. For every celebration, the decor, activities and gifts complemented the theme. Table mats, storytelling and games became staples, creating memories that lasted beyond the special day.

Then came his 11th birthday, and the Chinese New Year inspired the theme around this time. The essence of these celebrations was always twofold: to impart learning and to ensure Vedant enjoyed the day thoroughly. We usually held the parties on Saturdays so that all his friends could attend, given that our house was quite far from Sishya and most of his friends resided near the school.

Vedant had three birthday celebrations every year. The first took place in Kolkata immediately after New Year's, when the entire family would reunite to celebrate my father's birthday on the 31st. This pre-celebration would be followed by Vedant's actual birthday on 9 January. This day was more of an intimate gathering with just his grandparents and us. I encouraged him to visit a school of underprivileged children to distribute sweets, snacks and books. The final celebration was with his school friends at our home, featuring a different theme every year. What a blessing!

◆

Growing up, Vedant received a lot of love from everyone and always reciprocated. He was adored by all who interacted with him. While he was still overweight, the ones who cherished him did not care for it. They always believed he would shed the extra weight as he would grow taller and enter his teens. With his active lifestyle and mindful eating, they trusted it was only a matter of time.

As Revered Mahātria says: 'Celebration is life.'

A mother celebrates every child, delving within herself to offer them her best. For me too, this journey with Vedant continues.

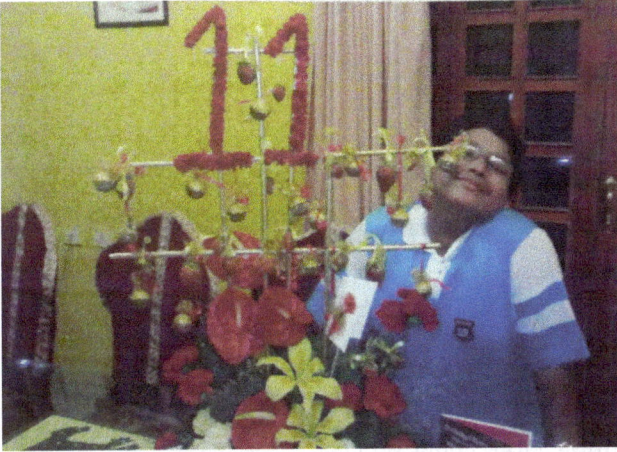

Vedant turns 11!

My Journey, My Life

My journey, my life—
To love all, and all the time.

We always speak about others;
Why? I often wonder.
When this life is my responsibility,
My *arpan* to my God,
Where no blaming is allowed.

Then why do we judge?
Why do we criticize?
Why do we form opinions?
Why, why, why?
I get muddled, my head reels.

I stop, I pause… I try to think;
Nay, I am unable to.
I complicate my life,
I make it difficult for myself,
As I move away from the centre.

Why the centre? They say that is where
God resides. 'Have you seen
Him, that you say so surely?'
Nay, I have not;
I have only felt Him when I love.

When I love everyone like He does,
When I see Him in everyone, as He sees us,
When I hold my little one and
Discover a new me; this is how I desire to
Make everyone feel—loved, loveable, loving.

I relate to my journey, my life, as
A mission to make all feel they, too, are in their
Mother's womb when they are with me.
They, too, are God's special one!
Like you, like me, like we all are.

My journey, my life—
To love all, and all the time.

Afterword

This is an unusual publication—an ode to motherhood—written by a loving daughter who, in praising her mother, reveals an inner depth that one would not suspect in the course of an everyday conversation with her. There are, no doubt, other loving daughters, but indeed very few who are able to express feelings about their mothers to this extent, almost elevating them to a kind of 'Mother Goddess'.

Manisha Kanoria Lohia's admiration for her mother and motherhood et al. comes through in every syllable of this brief publication, reflecting the deep spiritual connection between them. Only a person who possesses certain innate qualities can produce a tome of this kind. I would, hence, urge this to be preferred reading for all young women who seek to become mothers in their time.

The author also attributes deep meanings to the book's title *Umbilically Yours*, which is again quite unlike titles chosen by other well-meaning authors. The book's contents coming straight from the heart, invest this slim publication with extraordinary importance, displaying innate wisdom about an everyday act of giving birth to another human being, and about the sacrifice that mothers make in the process. This is, hence, an extraordinary presentation that imparts a mystic quality to motherhood and the birth of a child.

M.K. Narayanan
Former Governor of West Bengal

Accolades and Appreciation for the Book

'May this book, flowing through Higher Spiritual Beings through her [the author], become a source of inspiration and transformation with Happiness and Joy for all the women and men who are privileged to read it [...] Dr Manisha's own umbilical connection with her greatly respected mother Champa devi [and] her journey as a Montessorian have played an important role in making her believe there is a privilege, which only a woman is blessed with and that is "MOTHERHOOD" [...] I wish dear Dr Manisha that her desire and aim in writing this book to inspire people to take on the role of responsible parenthood is fulfilled.'

—Dame Dr Prof. Meher Master-Moos
Founder President, Zoroastrian College, Sanjan

'It was a pure delight to read and feel your words of love and affection towards motherhood, Manisha! Having been in the field of infertility practice for over 20 years, I have clearly seen and witnessed the hurt and heartbreak women endure due to infertility. I have also seen how their world dramatically transforms after their bundle of joy arrives home. Your decision to write a handbook on this beautiful journey of motherhood is simply superb [...] The title *Umbilically Yours* is so apt and perfectly captures the emotions you have so eloquently expressed [...] May this book serve as a guide, mentor and role model to all the expecting mothers, and may it gift them happiness and joy as well!'

—Dr Asha Vijay
Founder and Medical Director of GarbhaGudi

'This book is not a mere string of words, but of Truth that Manisha has lived by. When Manisha started writing this book, I had just conceived. I would eagerly look forward to reading the chapters she sent me—not just as an author–mentor but more as a mother-to-be […] I found peace in Manisha's words because I knew they came straight from the heart of a mother who had been through it all […] What most appealed to me is the honesty with which she has tackled every incident […] This book is a must-read for to-be mothers and mothers who will sometimes find themselves smiling, sometimes nodding and mostly just thinking, "Oh, so someone else too went through it all, and I am doing okay!"

I wish Manisha many more books, and experiences, so she can keep empowering her readers.'

—**Megha Bajaj**
Bestselling Author, TEDx Speaker, Author–Mentor,
Educator, Seeker and Founder, Wonders of Words

'Manisha makes everyone feel special. Her unconditional love, helping nature, soft ways and deep surrender and faith in her spiritual guru, Mahātria, make her truly one of a kind. One person whom Manisha absolutely adores is her mother, whose influence continues to shape her values, attitudes and personality […] When Manisha became a mother herself, the cycle of love, nurturing and growth continued, as she passed on her wisdom, values and traditions to her son, Vedant […] This book is all about the profound and eternal bond between a mother and child […] Every mother-to-be should have this book as a guide to understand the transformative power of motherhood.'

—**Chitra Prasad**
Author, Blogger, Seeker and
Correspondent, NSN Group of Schools

'The relationship between a mother and child is one of the most profound and sacred bonds in existence [...] *Umbilically Yours* is not just a tribute to mothers but an invitation to reflect on the universal essence of motherhood—one that is woven into our existence, whether we are children, mothers or even those who may never experience motherhood first-hand [...] Through her reflections, Manisha Kanoria Lohia's highlights the delicate interplay between inherited wisdom, personal experiences and the innate instincts that emerge when one steps into motherhood [...] The author's words carry an authenticity that can only come from deep personal experience and introspection. It is a celebration of *Janani*—the Sanskrit word for mother, the ultimate nurturer [...] This book is an ode to every mother, a tribute to their selfless love, and a reminder that no matter how far we go in life, we will always remain *Umbilically Yours*.'

—Dr Markandey Rai
Chairman, Global Peace Foundation (GPF) India
President, Indo-Pacific Peace Forum

'*Umbilically Yours* is more than a book—it is a soulful offering from a woman who lives motherhood every single day with awareness, grace and purpose. Manisha Lohia is not only a devoted mother but also a thoughtful Montessori educator whose gentle strength, deep sensitivity and rooted values reflect in every page. The concept of *Seeing, Becoming and Being* a mother is a powerful and evocative lens through which she invites us to explore the emotional, spiritual and practical journey of womanhood. This book is a heartfelt tribute to the timeless bond between mother and child—a gift to every woman, whether she is contemplating motherhood, living it or simply seeking to reconnect with the sacred essence of *Janani*.'

—Gita Krishna Raj
National Head of Physical Education Program
for Schools (PEPS), Sports Sector Skill Council of India

'Reading *Umbilically Yours* felt like returning to a space filled with tenderness, quiet wisdom and the gentle strength only a mother brings. Written by someone who has been a maternal presence in my life, it's a book that is both deeply personal and universally moving. Coming from an education and development background, I was struck by how seamlessly it blends lived experience, Montessori philosophy and emotional depth. The book goes beyond biology, inviting us to reflect on how we see, become and hold space as nurturers in all forms. With the insight of someone who has guided generations through her Montessori school, Manisha Lohia brings empathy, intuition and understanding to every page. *Umbilically Yours* is for mothers, daughters, educators and all who are drawn to the quiet power of maternal love.'

—Meenakshi Krishnaraj
Associate Director, Maverick Fitness & Beyond

'A mother's relationship with her child is special—pure and beautiful—and her love is unconditional […] Manisha Kanoria Lohia examine this relationship in great depth, drawing on her experience as a child, a mother and a Montessori Educator. This is a wonderful book from which we can all learn something from […] I highly recommend *Umbilically Yours* to all parents.'

—Ranjit Chaudhri
National Bestselling Author

'In an age when several Indian youth are confused and caught up in myriad emotions, comes a refreshing break in the form of a book titled *Umbilically Yours*, authored by Manisha Kanoria Lohia. While it covers a plethora of subjects and issues, the book's central theme is based on the joy and privilege a woman is bestowed with on becoming a mother […] She has singled out the three sections of seeing, becoming and being a mother, and has dwelled on the bond and relationship between young girls and their mothers […] Her goal was for this book to become a handbook for all

mothers or mothers-to-be, who seek living a holistic and spiritual life [...] *Umbilically Yours* is truly a commendable literary effort.'
—Inder Raj Ahluwalia
Travel Journalist and Author

'What a beautiful and heartfelt narration. *Umbilically Yours* is a tribute from one mother to another—written with tenderness, honesty and the kind of unspoken understanding that only motherhood can inspire. It captures the essence of this life-altering journey in a way that feels both deeply personal and universally resonant.

Congratulations, Manisha, on creating a work of such depth and grace. This is not just a book—it's a companion every would-be mother deserves by her side. I'm honoured to be among its early readers and look forward to many more such gems from you.'
—Jayan Narayanan
Founder, Toss the coin and Co-founder, Jokesapart

'*Umbilically Yours* is a book *of* the mothers, *by* a mother—but not just *for* the mothers. That's what I call deMOMcracy. The author knows so much about mothers and motherhood—clearly, she's a MOMtessori educator in the school of life. I have no doubt this book will become the *mother* of all reading experiences.'
—Sridhar Ranganathan
Co-founder, Jokesapart

In Gratitude

To my Mahātria, who has guided me deeper within, in my connection to my FAITH.

To Dr A.P.J. Abdul Kalam, whose love for children and youth ignited a desire in me to play my part.

To M.K. Narayanan, former Governor of West Bengal, for his unwavering support of my vision and ambition in developing young minds.

To my Maa, Papa, Hemant and Sanjeev for being my constant source of inspiration.

To my husband, whose unconditional support made the journey of writing this book seamless.

To my niece, nephews and all the children I have been blessed to interact with from a young age.

To my son, who has given me the invaluable experience of holding him within, sparking the truest feelings and emotions of motherhood.

To all my teachers and mentors, especially Mrs Sukanya Raghavan, my Montessori teacher, for being my guiding light.

To Megha, my mentor, who helped bring this book to life.

To my dearest friend and brother, Sridhar Ranganathan, who believes in the immense potential this book holds for everyone.

To my very close friend and yoga lover, Shoba, whose guidance has deepened my connection with God through her voice as she guides me through practices.

To everyone at Rupa Publications who helped facilitate this book.

There are so many things I wonder about
You as you grow inside me. I wonder when
I will get to meet you; I wonder who you will take after.
But one thing I never wonder is how much
I love you or will love you.
Because I know—you are my everything.
I am in awe of the very feeling of motherhood.
As a mother, I truly feel blessed to have been chosen by
God to carry another life within me. The very feeling
Of having a life within, makes me feel so responsible.
It feels as if someone is always watching, observing
And getting acquainted with everything of me, so I
Better be careful of my thoughts, words and actions.

www.ingramcontent.com/pod-product-compliance
Lightning Source LLC
Chambersburg PA
CBHW060416100426
42812CB00037B/3484/J